Tarot
Inspired
Life

© Christy Carr

About the Author

Jaymi Elford views tarot as a tool to create meaning and explore the world we live in. She's been slinging cards since she was young—a deck is always close. Beyond authoring numerous books and decks, she teaches and discusses innovative divination techniques at conferences across North America, and online on popular podcasts. She lives in Portland, Oregon and would love for you to visit her at www.innercompasstarot.com.

JAYMI ELFORD

Tarot
Inspired
Life

Use *the* Cards
to Enhance
your Life

Llewellyn Worldwide
Woodbury, Minnesota

FIRST EDITION
Second Printing, 2021

Book design by Bob Gaul
Cover design by Shira Atakpu
Editing by Laura Kurtz
Interior tarot spreads by Llewellyn Art Department
Card images on cover from *Triple Goddess Tarot* courtesy of Lo Scarabeo

Llewellyn Publications is a registered trademark of Llewellyn Worldwide Ltd.

Library of Congress Cataloging-in-Publication Data

Name: Elford, Jaymi, author.
Title: Tarot inspired life : use the cards to enhance your life / Jaymi Elford.
Description: First Edition. | Woodbury : Llewellyn Worldwide, Ltd., 2019. |
    Includes bibliographical references.
Identifiers: LCCN 2018044020 (print) | LCCN 2018048331 (ebook) | ISBN
    9780738760001 (ebook) | ISBN 9780738759944 (alk. paper)
Subjects: LCSH: Tarot.
Classification: LCC BF1879.T2 (ebook) | LCC BF1879.T2 E457 2019 (print) |
    DDC 133.3/2424—dc23
LC record available at https://lccn.loc.gov/2018044020

Llewellyn Publications
A Division of Llewellyn Worldwide Ltd.
2143 Wooddale Drive
Woodbury, MN 55125-2989
www.llewellyn.com

Printed in the United States of America

Contents

Exercise List

Acknowledgments

First and foremost, thanks to my partner, Kender Elford. Without you, this book wouldn't have manifested. You gave me the time, space, and push to chase my dreams. OMG, I did it, babe.

I also want to thank my team of readers and editors: Anna Alexander, Barbara Moore, and Laura Kurtz. Thanks for reading and re-reading all this, patiently working through the exercises. You are awesome; your insights and thoughts strengthened and organized my ideas.

Finally, I want to thank my tarot tribe of friends and teachers, among them Melissa Cynova, Hilary Parry, Andrew MacGregor, Theresa Reed, Rose Red and Andrew Robinson, Benebell Wen, and everyone else. Your knowledge, insight, gentle patience, and guidance made me the reader I am today. Thank you for fueling my passion for tarot and giving me limitless ways to use the cards.

Author's Note

Welcome aboard! Tarot isn't just a pack of cards used for divining futures. It's a fabulous tool for examining your inner and outer worlds. Tarot can bring peace into your life when it spins out of control. It can help you make better decisions by showing you what actions and paths to take. Tarot has the power to change your life, once you learn how to crack the shell of the nut and get inside, down to the kernel of what it has to offer.

Already familiar with the cards? No problem. *Tarot Inspired Life* includes experiments and ideas to expand your knowledge. Use this book along with your favorite deck as a laboratory manual to explore new ways of using your favorite deck.

I wrote *Tarot Inspired Life* for you to connect to a tarot deck in a personalized way. I won't ask you to memorize lists of keywords. Instead, I will ask you to look at the cards and focus on how they tie into your life, your culture, and your passions. I give you permission to delve into using the cards outside the norm. The ideas in this book may also challenge what you know about tarot.

The power of tarot may or may not give you profound life changes, but it can help you dig deeper into uncovering who you are and what purposes you have to offer in this lifetime.

I believe anyone can learn to use the cards and harness their power with only the help of their mind, memories, and a paper and pen. If you have those, you are ready to experience the world of tarot and create your own tarot inspired life.

For more insights, visit the companion website:

www.tarotinspiredlife.com

Introduction

Welcome to the *Tarot Inspired Life* laboratory.

Your laboratory is a safe and sacred place to learn about, study, play, and experiment with the divination tool known as the tarot. I hereby give you permission to use the cards in ways you might have not thought about before. As you go through this book, open your mind to all possibilities. All ideas count. Everything is a clue, a link that merits exploration. There is no right or wrong.

Each chapter groups tarot exercises around a central theme. What you should take away from each chapter is clearly stated in the beginning. Section one helps you gain the basics of tarot. You'll learn history, how to get your first deck, and ways to explore the cards and make your own meanings. Section two breaks out of the traditional divination mold. Explore your creative side, learn how to do invocations and perform seasonal rituals, and use the deck as a way to get in touch with your spirit helpers. Section three guides you into connecting with the larger tarot community. All the items in these later chapters can be retooled to fit your passions, your spirituality, and your lifestyle. Not interested in a particular chapter? Skip it.

New to tarot? Read this book from the first chapter to the last. It gently introduces you to the seventy-eight-card deck: its history and myths; its structure; and how you can create your own tarot meanings to connect to each card.

Advanced students, get out of your rut and use the book as your divination guide. Pick a random spot and see where it (and your deck) takes you.

Enjoy the time spent in your tarot lab. For those new to tarot, let this book teach you an appreciation for the cards—you'll find that once you start, you'll have a life-long relationship. For the more experienced readers, may *Tarot Inspired Life* break you out of your comfort zone—to jumpstart your own discoveries on how the cards can impact your life.

In order to perform the exercises in this book, you'll need the following items:

- **A journal.** Record the exercises and thoughts you have on the cards with your journal. Use inspiring mediums, whether a bound book or digital. Composition notebooks work great. They're inexpensive and large enough to carry in a bag but not as intimidating as some journals. They come in a wide range of paper types and can be found in most grocery stores. While you can use your computer to record your thoughts, computers have many distractions, attracting our inner magpie.

- **A pen.** Use a pen to jot down your thoughts. Pens are better than pencils because ink is permanent. Pencils tempt your inner editor to erase what you wrote and start over. When you use a pen, however, there is no temptation and you have to record ideas as they come to you. If you like, keep a variety of colored pens nearby. You can create a color coded key to track your progress through this book. Use a black pen to record the first time you encounter an experiment. Later on, you can use a blue pen to add new impressions when you revisit older notes, and so on. It's all up to you and how you learn best, but stick with using a pen. If you're keeping electronic records, try using different fonts or colors to manage your information.

- **A tarot deck.** You'll need one or two basic tarot decks for the exercises. Select a deck with illustrations on each and every card, as not all tarot decks do this; many display pips on the minor arcana. Thankfully, there's a lot of decks out there so you can select from a wide variety of art styles, themes, and card sizes.

Got all the materials? Awesome. Turn the page and let's get started.

Part 1
What Tarot Is

Chapter 1

History and Structure

By the end of this chapter you'll:

- Learn myths and history

- Understand basic structure

- Discover how tarot works

Tarot is full of myths and urban legends. There are myths about who gets to touch the cards. There are myths about who can buy decks for interested students. There are even stories surrounding how to store your cards when not in use. People know more old wives' tales surrounding tarot than about the cards themselves, and I think there may actually be more myths out there on where tarot came from and who created the cards than actual factual history. Thanks to many great historical books on tarot, we can separate fact from fiction. Here are some of my favorite myths.

Used by Roma people. This is an ever-popular myth. I can't recall where I first heard this, but one book said "Gypsies" (the Romani, or Roma people) created the cards as a way to communicate with foreign peoples. They would lay down cards like a picture book to suggest what they wanted to say. Those they dealt with would look at these pictures to understand what was needed. Then they'd use the rest of the deck to craft their response. Coming from an anthropological background, tarot being used as a powerful, universal translator sparked my imagination. It remains one of my favorite myths.

Created by Egyptians. An occultist named Antoine Court de Gébelin connected tarot to the Egyptian god Thoth, the god of communication and magic, as well as the creator of alchemy. Thoth's worshippers put all his teachings into a book that could shift and change, much like the god himself. Over the years, the followers of Thoth roamed the lands and became known as Gypsies. They would use the cards to share the wisdom of Thoth. The ability to shuffle and reorder the texts helped obfuscate the true book's order, so non-believers couldn't decipher Thoth's messages.

Last remaining Atlantis artifact. The Atlanteans created tarot as a way to impart wisdom and knowledge of their culture. As their culture lay dying and their city sinking, some Atlanteans didn't want this wisdom to pass into the watery grave along with the rest of the items they created. Someone escaped the sinking city with the cards and shared them with the rest of the world.

Myths about tarot's origins aren't the only stories in town. Many decks have their own stories and vast worlds created within them. There are decks created with specific fantasy stories in mind, and others dive deeper into the mythology of cultures from around our world. Every deck I have come across tends to have its own voice and story written in the images (and in some cases, in the booklets); all you have to do is look for the patterns.

Card images draw our sense of curiosity in, just like the wondrous creatures and heroes found inside a myth. Tarot's imagery speaks to the part of our brain that creates meaning, and we crave making meaning. We ask, "What does it mean?"

We study and read myths first because at its core tarot tells stories. The images evoke emotion. In turn, this allows us to blend intuition and creativity to craft meaning. Essentially, laying cards down and creating meaning from spreads are a lot like reading well-written myths. Both forms of communication capture our imagination. Myths and tarot imagery are built off a symbolic language which excites the right side of our brain. We are seekers—looking to make meaning from situations and people we meet every day. Mythology and tarot, then, are two ways we have to help us determine our origins and how we fit into this crazy world we call Earth. We're hardwired to do this.

Selected Moments from Tarot History

The real history of the cards isn't as glamorous as the myths portray. The history of the tarot spans many centuries and several cultures. Don't worry, I don't expect you to remember a long list of dates or events. There's no quiz waiting for you at the end of the book.

The first stop on our tour takes us to the second century CE where playing cards and paper were invented in China. In these early days, cards had human figures, mostly of royalty or other important figures painted on them. The cards were traded along the Silk Road routes, which is important because it brought the idea of cards and using them for games to other cultures throughout Asia and Europe.

Tarot decks, with their distinct structure, first appeared in Italy around the 1400s. One of the few surviving decks from this era, the Visconti, was created around the 1420s. Visiting Italy? Don't forget to look up museums carrying some of the original cards. Tarot decks during this time were used to play a popular game called *tarocchi*. However, only the wealthy and nobles could afford decks at this time; handmade decks were given as gifts for important anniversaries.

In 1781, de Gébelin claimed tarot came from Egypt. While we know the Egyptian connection is an origin myth, this becomes tarot's first connection to spiritual and occult lore.

Move forward to 1910, the year the first popular, mass-produced, and standardized tarot deck was released. Arthur Edward (A. E.) Waite, member of the famous Golden Dawn occult society, commissioned Pamela Colman Smith to illustrate the deck. Waite sold the deck to the Rider company, which printed and sold the deck globally. People all over the world could now use the deck to tell fortunes and divine futures. The companion book *Spiritual Keys to the Tarot* introduced the Celtic Cross spread.

Then in 1944, Aleister Crowley created his own tarot, called the Thoth deck. Heavily influenced by Egyptian lore, he fashioned the deck in homage to Thoth. His version became popular, and many decks today use Crowley's structure of the major arcana.

We can trace most of the current and modern decks back to either the Rider-Waite-Smith or Crowley decks, though not all tarot decks have the same system. If you lay out the major arcana of each system side by side, you will notice a few differences. The first comes out in the order of the cards. In the Rider-Waite-Smith deck, card eight is named Strength, and card eleven is Justice. While Crowley was a member of the Golden Dawn, he had creative differences and his own ideas for the deck's structure. When it was time to release his own deck, Crowley switched Strength and Justice to suit his own view of the world.

Many people may not care to know which branch of the tarot tree their deck lands on, though learning history does add some depth and layers to the tool. Getting to know a deck on a deeper level helps you examine others' perspectives and why they use the systems they choose. Researching information about a deck's creator and how they developed your deck gives more insight into why symbols appear on various cards. Tarot is a flexible tool you can use to tap into both the rich history and your own personal perspective.

Today, the world has seen a huge explosion of new decks that feature just about any sort of pantheon or cultural mix. From art deco artwork to watercolor fantasy paint-scapes, anyone interested in acquiring a deck can find one to tickle their fancy. We're even seeing the birth of eDecks, electronic tarot apps for mobile devices. Only time will tell what future tarot innovations await us.

A Brief Guide to Tarot Structure

Tarot is an elegant cartomancy system. Cartomancy is just fancy word meaning "divination by cards." There are many types of cartomancy-style decks out there these days, including: playing cards, Lenormand, and other oracle systems. How does one tell tarot apart from all the other oracle decks? We look at the structure of the deck. Tarot has a specific structure: seventy-eight cards broken down into five suits. Other oracle decks contain more or fewer cards than this. If the deck you have doesn't have this structure, it is not a tarot deck—it's an oracle.

As a tool, tarot was well designed and thought out. The Golden Dawn used their tarot system to help their members delve deeper into their studies. Each symbol, color choice, and image was carefully plotted and drawn. Each object on the card has special meanings designed to clue the reader in to what the card meant and how it related to the question at hand.

Tarot structure also shows a particular cosmology of the energies going into the birth of the universe. Tarot contains five elemental associations, and four worlds. When you lay out all the cards in a particular pattern, it shows you how the universe was made and how everything in the universe can fit into the cards. Thinking about this blows my mind. You will see glimpses of this philosophy later in the book and as you continue studying tarot on your own.

Parts of a Tarot Deck

Tarot has three parts: a major arcana containing twenty-two cards, a minor arcana containing forty-two numbered cards, and fourteen court cards. The court cards are also a part of the minor arcana, thus bringing the total numbers of minor arcana cards to fifty-six. We will discuss each part in the following sections.

Major Arcana

When you open a pack of tarot cards for the first time, usually the first card in the pack has a name on it—the Fool. This is followed by twenty-one other cards with names. Together these twenty-two cards are collectively called the major arcana.

Arcana is Latin for "secrets" and these twenty-two cards represent common and global archetypes. These archetypes show the human condition as it moves across the spiritual state of the universe. The major arcana also uses a unique numbering system, as it begins at card zero with the Fool and ends at card twenty-one, the World. The major arcana belong to the element of aether, or spirit, for the cards represent aspects inside all of us.

Above all, the majors tell a story. We call this story *the Fool's Journey,* for the cards numbered one to twenty-two become the chapters in which the Fool (0) travels.

Archetypes

An archetype is a universally understood template made of patterns and behaviors that transcend cultural norms. These images shape many aspects of life from characters in stories to personality traits. We emulate and aspire to bring in qualities of archetypes we're drawn to. We also have the innate ability to recognize and interpret their meanings.

In tarot, archetypes play a huge role in the organization of the major arcana. In fact, each card contains a distinct archetype. Tarot is a symbolic language; as such, archetypes become a perfect mechanism to bring forth a symbolic discussion between ourselves and the cards. Knowing tarot archetypes helps us learn more about ourselves, the people we care for, and the human condition.

The following list gives you my interpretation of the archetypes found in each major arcana card:

The Fool: The child. The Fool represents the innocence and wonder of a child, an individual being born into the world who learns how to navigate the world. The Fool experiences life through the beginner's mind lens. Each escapade is new; he sees the world with clear eyes and explores the world free from restraints.

The Magician: The divine masculine. The Magician represents the masculine or external side of a person. This energy allows us to discover what we excel at. Once we know this, we're able to communicate our visions to others and can set those plans into motion. The Magician takes ideas from his imagination and manifests them into our physical reality.

The High Priestess: The divine feminine. The High Priestess represents the feminine or internal side of a person. From this archetype we learn about the power of being still and accessing our intuition. The High Priestess listens to the currents of the universe and allows those hints to guide and teach.

The Empress: The mother. The Empress expresses the traits of a loving and nurturing caretaker who is also creative and abundant. We tap into this energy when we get our needs met, sustain ourselves, and allow abundance into our life. As such, many decks depict the figure on this card as either an aspect of a living Earth, or pregnant and close to giving birth.

The Emperor: The father. The Emperor displays power and authority. We use the structure of this archetype to set boundaries, routines, and focus. Achievement comes from being able to set clear intentions. His limitations help us understand what we are capable of and how we can push beyond them.

The Hierophant: The teacher. Many people view the Hierophant as embodying the spirit of structured religion and dogmatic beliefs. Lately, I've come to view the Hierophant as a teacher, one who guides us out of ignorance so we can navigate the world and life's challenges. He reveals patterns so we can understand what is best for our own mind, body, and spirit.

The Lovers: Connection. The Lovers represents the universal desire to connect with others. Love and desire are powerful emotions that influence our interpersonal connections. We spend much of our lives seeking others to associate with. When we discover others whose interests intersect with ours, the bonds influence our lives in amazing ways.

The Chariot: Momentum. Chariots are vehicles designed to get riders from one place to another. Charioteers use reins to send signals to the horses attached. These subtle movements route the chariot to the desired location. Ironically, many chariot card designs depict the image of a charioteer and the vehicle at rest, sometimes without wheels. We are then led to believe the propulsion system used comes directly from the charioteer's mind. As a representative of momentum, the Chariot urges us to pursue our dreams.

Strength: Endurance. Strength shows us the importance of human determination. No matter how dark the situation gets, or where we are, we endure and can flourish despite setbacks.

The Hermit: Wisdom. The Hermit represents the archetype of wisdom. Wisdom is not easily earned, it's a process. It happens when one takes knowledge and applies personal insight to transform it. Wisdom comes when one sits still to absorb and process lessons and information life delivers. Once we integrate what we've learned, we can turn back to the outside to share the wisdom. This action is shown in the Hermit's lantern, which shines brightly to attract others to hear what he has to say.

The Wheel of Fortune: Fate/Destiny. The Wheel of Fortune contains the cycles of Earth. Spring, summer, autumn, and winter, the world turns and ages through time. These cycles influence us; we are intertwined. The Wheel of Fortune displays the universe's rhythms. We are at its whims. The universe has a single constant of change. It moves in circles.

Justice: Morality. This archetype deals with acceptable and unacceptable actions in society. Each culture has its own moral codes that dictate how to be a healthy, contributing member of the society. Justice shows how well we've integrated these rules and whether or not society responds in kind.

The Hanged Man: Sacrifice. Life is filled with choices, for every turn we take, we leave behind an alternative path. We surrender ourselves, items we own, and ideals to receive something better. The Hanged Man tells us to let go of outdated perspectives so we can receive new observations. Doing so can lead us to a better understanding of the world.

Death: Death and Rebirth. Many people view death as the end of an experience. In the tarot, Death represents a release of old ways, a sloughing off of what we no longer need, in order to make way for the new. It is a card of powerful transitions.

Temperance: Equilibrium. In this card, we learn the path of stability: the powerful force of blending two perspectives, or possibilities, together so we can find balance in our life.

The Devil: The Trickster. Tricksters are playful characters who live outside traditional behaviors and norms. They find themselves in seemingly impossible situations with no chance of escape and then, somehow, they miracu-lously escape with little exertion. The Devil as a trickster figure says being stuck is an illusion and the way out is usually easier than we think.

The Tower: Chaos. Change is a universal constant. When chaos strikes, it knocks us off our feet unexpectedly. Unwanted change throws us off balance and puts us into a tailspin that forces us to figure a solution or a way out. Sometimes having our world turned upside down gives us clarity and a fresh start.

The Star: Hope. When we look to the stars, we see hope. The stars always shine, and our lives do get better. Without hope, life seems meaningless and trudging through the daily grind becomes too much.

The Moon: Illusion. The light of the moon casts shadows and brings out the spooky vibes in our lives. As an arche-type, the Moon masks the truth of a situation and causes doubt. The Moon has been a symbol of mystery and emotional instability for mankind.

The Sun: Enlightenment. The Sun reminds us of the people, experiences, and physical pleasures warming our heart and bringing us joy and happiness. The Sun feeds us and helps keep us alive by providing our bodies with heat and sources of vitamins.

Judgment: Awakening. Judgement brings us to a new calling. We have worked hard to know ourselves, to beat the illusions and negative habits. Now we are free to start anew. We rise up, push beyond what we know, and head into the unknown with a renewed sense of direction. Images on Judgement remind us of the Biblical Judgment Day where the spirits rise up from their slumber and are released.

The World: Reunion. We come to the last card, the World (sometimes the Universe). The World represents the promise of return. When we die, we are reunited with those who came before us. It also represents another cycle in life: birth, death, rebirth.

Introduction to the Fool's Journey

The Fool's Journey is a mythic story-telling device that explores the interconnections and meanings within the twenty-two major arcana cards. In this framework, the Fool (0) becomes the main character in a story. This story follows who the Fool meets, locations he visits, and activities he participates in during his travels throughout the cards. If you go online, you can find many interpretations of the Fool's Journey. Below is an example of a Fool's Journey from the Fool (0) to the Lovers (IV).

Once upon a time there was a Fool who set out for adventure with only what he could carry on his back. With his head high in the clouds, he walks toward a cliff, unaware of the danger he faces. His small companion, a white dog, barks at his heels.

Descending from the cliffs, the Fool wanders into a lavish garden filled with roses and lilies and crawling vines. A man, the Magician, stands in the center. His red robes ruffle in a gentle breeze. His gaze rests upon the table in front of him, on which lie four implements. Celestial power flows from his hands to his head and a halo appears. The Fool, mesmerized, wants to learn all he can from this strong and self-confident being. So, the Magician takes the Fool on as his apprentice and teaches him the ways of manifestation: mastering the art of magic through using the wand, sword, chalice, and pentacles.

Armed with the tools of the Magician, the Fool wanders along his path. Daytime changes to night and he comes upon a beautiful lady sitting between two pillars. She cradles a set of scrolls in her lap. She lifts her head up and smiles at the Fool. He bends down and sits next to her. She lays her hand on his head as they sit in silence. While the Fool is confused, he understands—more lessons are taking place. He closes his eyes and taps into his intuition. His inner guides begin talking. As the first rays of sunlight appear, the Fool bows in gratitude and takes his leave.

As the day progresses, the Fool stumbles into a forest. Sitting under the warm rays of sunlight sits a voluptuous woman. She rests her back against a chaise lounge. Her golden locks frame her round, smiling face. The Fool inhales the fresh morning air. She weaves a story of her empire, for she is the Empress, and invites him to stay for a meal. They chat about his past and he shows her his tools; she says they'll help him manifest his creative desires. She shares the abundance of the forest with the Fool before he leaves.

Trees give way to sand and dust. The Fool stumbles out from the dunes and comes face to face with a tall man on his throne. His well-worn armor glints from years of use. This Emperor points down at the Fool and recounts the rules and laws of the land which the Fool must obey. Despite being told about various limitations, the Fool feels quite free to explore. The Fool learns how having defined boundaries frees him to move around. He obeys the laws while traveling in the Emperor's lands and continues on his merry way.

The sounds of bells draw the Fool to a church. Golden bells atop the steeple ring loud and clear, drawing parishioners to the building. He enters the church and meets the Hierophant, a man sitting in a chair flanked by two attendees. The Hierophant sees the innocence in the Fool and bids him forward to receive a blessing. The Hierophant raises his hand high and imbues the Fool with understanding of a greater force. Inspired with this teaching, the Fool moves ever forward.

Soon he comes across a strange scene: two people stand naked, holding hands, as an angel hovers over them. The Fool bears witness to a ceremony. After the proceedings, he learns how these Lovers are choosing to spend their lives together, to be as one unit. They teach him what it takes to be a good partner, if he ever chooses to connect to another spirit in this way. He hugs them all and adds the knowledge they taught him about love and choice into the bag with his other belongings.

The idea of the Fool's Journey is an important teaching tool to tarot, because with it we learn how to craft stories. Every time you lay cards down for a reading you are crafting a story, or having one told to you. Knowing how to blend one card into another helps your skills as a storyteller grow and improve. Writing your own Fool's Journey is a good exercise to do because it helps you build your own mythology with your tarot deck.

EXERCISE: THE MAJORS MATRIX

I put my students through this exercise when they first come to me. With just the major arcana, you can see how all twenty-one cards flow into the story we know as the Fool's Journey. It allows for cross-examination of the archetypes, colors, and meanings contained in each image. It's also a great exercise for doing deck comparison with multiple decks.

Each row of the matrix shows you a level of human experience and consciousness. Row one embodies human dependence, or how human consciousness requires an outside hand to lean on while we grow. Row two shows how an individual learns to become independent and self-reliant. The final row demonstrates the inter-dependence of our consciousness, as we move from being reliant on ourselves to becoming an interconnected part of society.

Another story woven into the matrix are the three stages of human development. Row one equals our childhood and how we learn about the world. Row two becomes our teen and young adult stage, where we learn to develop relationships and define our place in the world. Row three defines the elder years, where we stop caring about the daily grind and focus on making peace with the world before we transition back into spirit.

Ready to construct your first matrix? Pull out all the major arcana cards from your deck. Put the rest of the deck aside; you won't need them yet. You may want to do this exercise on the floor or on a table with space.

Place the Fool in front of you. Since this card begins with zero, we typically consider it outside the sequence for reasons you'll see.

Drop down one row and place card numbers one to seven in sequential order. Drop one more row down and place card numbers eight to fourteen down. You'll place one more row of seven using the remaining cards (fifteen through twenty-one).

Your completed matrix should look like the image below:

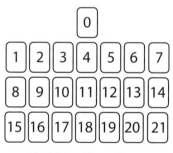

The Majors Matrix Layout

Once you've finished constructing your own matrix, take out your journal and answer the following questions:

- What similarities and differences do the cards in each row have?

- What similarities and differences to the cards in each column have?

- What overall story is told in the images?

- Do you see color patterns in the rows or columns?

Minor Arcana

The minor arcana is made up of four suits: wands, swords, cups, and pentacles—ten cards in each suit. The images drawn on these cards relate to aspects of our daily life. The numbering on the suits starts with Ace (as number one) and counts up to ten. These cards give the what, where, and when aspects of a reading. Each suit has many connections to one of the four elements. Each suit is said to depict the cardinal medieval virtues: justice, wisdom, courage, and temperance. The suits also correspond to various universal truths such as: self and identity; how one relates to others; communication and beliefs; and the physical world and items within it that make us feel secure.

In the cosmic tale of the universe's creation, the minor arcana represent the ten stages of how our world and items within are created from a single idea, to the action behind its manifestation, to the emotional connection, and then, to making it manifest in the physical world. We'll explore this idea more fully in the next four sections when we meet the four suit families.

While I have written about the four suits of the minor arcana using names and symbols I am familiar with, not all tarot decks use the same imagery for each suit. Some decks contain variants on their suits such as stones, rods, coins, staves, and so on. When you purchase your own deck, spend some time with its booklet to understand what the symbols represent.

Some decks also switch their elemental associations between the swords and wands suits. Swords become fire and wands air. Many friends use this division because they see swords as aggressive tools and wands as intellect based. There are many reasons why someone would want to switch them; for example, swords are used as weapons and fire is typically seen as an emotion which riles us up and enrages us. Wands, by contrast, are used to put our ideas into creation: tooling statues or becoming the legs of a chair. No matter what side of the swords and wands debate you fall on, the cards will still work for you in the way you want them to work.

The Swords

This suit features images of people holding swords, carrying them, or being contained or boxed in by them. Swords relates to the element of air. As representations of air, they tell stories based around ideas, challenges and conflicts, and communication.

The swords are the first to hit the stage of universal creation. In order to manifest our desires—a star, a planet, your goals—you must first have an idea of what it is you want to summon. This idea springs forth from our minds and uses the energy of all ten cards in the swords suit, from the Ace's powerful kernel of creation to the Ten's death of the idea itself.

The Wands

This suit depicts people using and wielding long sticks. Wands relate to the element of fire. As a representation of fire, they show us scenes of making our passions alive—what we're willing to defend, what makes us excited, and how we utilize our creativity.

The wands are the second to hit the stage of universal creation. Now that we have an idea of what we want to manifest, it's time to set the plan into motion with action. We chop wood and make a fire. We tend to the fire and use it to construct food or tools. The ten cards of this suit show how the flames of fire grow from a tiny seed to a brightly burning bonfire ready to heat up our creation.

The Cups

The cups show scenes of people looking at or holding cups. This suit relates to the element of water. Overall, this suit shows our emotional landscape—how we view relationships with others, how we contain our feelings when they aren't meant to be put into a shape, and situations that ebb and flow like water in our lives.

The cups are the third to hit the stage of universal creation. Once our fire burns steadily, we can use the water to fuel our emotions to get the right mix of emotion and flow for what we are manifesting. Water tempers and balances the fire's heat. Too much fire and we become too focused on what we're creating. Too much water and we get too emotionally attached. The ten cards in this suit show how our emotions flow from a drop to a watery cascade of feelings for our creation.

The Pentacles

Last but not least are the pentacles. This suit is named for the disks or coins with a five-pointed star drawn on them. These cards depict people working with or reaching out for the pentacles. Pentacles relate to the element of earth. They show us how material possessions, our home life, and our work/careers provide us with the stability we seek.

In our path to universal manifestation, the pentacles display the culmination of all the prior three suits' efforts. At this stage, the physical manifestation of the dream becomes real and takes form. We successfully took our dream through the four steps of creation from getting an idea in our minds to fanning it with the flames of desire and tempering it with our watery emotions. The item we've dreamed up is now ready for us to touch and enjoy.

Exercise: The Minors Matrix

We can lay out the minor arcana cards just like we did the major arcana. For this experiment, remove the Ace through the Ten from each of the four suits. Each suit gets laid out in its own row: swords, wands, cups, and pentacles. Your grid should look like this image:

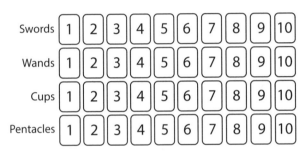

The Minors Matrix Layout

The stories unfolding in the Minors Matrix are taught in fours. They tell the stories of the seasons and their shifts from one to the other; they represent the four cardinal directions; the steps in the process to manifest our desires; and the four stages of life from birth, childhood, adulthood, and old age. And as a boon for us pagans, they also represent the four tenets of the Witches' Pyramid: to know, to will, to dare, and to keep silent.

Once you've finished constructing your own matrix, take out your journal and answer the following questions:

- What similarities and differences do the cards in each row have?

- What similarities and differences to the cards in each column have?

- What overall story is told in the images?

- Do you see color patterns in the rows or columns?

Court Cards

The court cards have a dualistic nature. They are part of the minor arcana because each suit has an associated court. Counted this way, it brings the minor arcana up to a total of fourteen cards. There are four cards in each court, so there are sixteen court cards total. Each court position also relates itself to one of the four elements: earth, air, fire, and water. Whereas the minor arcana cards represent the what, where, and when of a reading, the court cards can become the whom of the reading. They can be aspects of yourself or they can embody others who appear in your life.

Instead of numbers, each court member has a title. Common titles include: page, knight, queen, and king. However, your court cards may have different names, such as princess, mother, father, son, and daughter. This book uses page, knight, queen, and king labels.

Pages

The pages are the messengers of the deck. They represent the youngest member at the court. As such, they are still learning the ropes of what it means to be the enlightened aspect of their element. Because of their apparent curiosity about the world around them and what knowledge they learn, the pages correspond to the element of air. Pages are said to represent the youthful energies of taking on a new station or interest in life. They have a certain air of confidence around them, for they are excited about the new position they are undertaking.

Knights

The knights are the movers and shakers of the court. They represent the riled up adolescent filled with action and energy. Knights are poised to pounce, to save the day and princesses from the psychic, physical, and emotional evils that have befallen them. Knights belong to the element of fire, for their passions and actions cause them to burn brightly. Knights are drawn in motion, they act swiftly and don't think about what they are going to do before they do it. They do it now and worry about the consequences later.

Queens

The queens are pillars of feminine confidence. These motherly figures sit in their stately positions and offer advice from growing close to their element. We relate the queens to water, for emotions swirl and run around them constantly. They show passion and emotion for their suit and everything they do. The queen can be calm one minute and ruthless the next, all depending on how you approach her and what wisdom she has to impart.

Kings

The kings are the heads of the household for each suit. They lead with a stable and strong rule. As rulers, they get called upon to settle disputes between their subjects. Because their high stature makes them such good leaders, the kings represent the rock solid element of earth. While appearing stoic, kings temper and balance their personal feelings in order to pass judgment when it is required of them.

Exercise: Court Card Matrix

Remove the sixteen court cards from your tarot deck and lay them out in the following Court Card Matrix grid. Start with the swords suit, then move on to wands, cups, and pentacles.

The Court Card Matrix Layout

Once you've finished constructing your own matrix, take out your journal and answer the following questions:

- Who does each person remind you of, living or fictitious? One of the best ways to learn the court is to create connections to people you know.

- How does each person in the court families relate to one another? Do they act as a cohesive family unit or can you feel the tension between each family member?

- What similarities do each of the pages, knights, queens, and kings have? How would each relate to one another in each suit?

- What differences do each have?

- Does color seem to play a special role in determining how you feel about each person in the card?

Introduction to the Grand Matrix

Up until now, you've been working with the smaller subsets of tarot. Looking at each subset familiarizes you with the larger archetypes and patterns found in the tarot. We start small because it's easier to work with a broad stroke before adding in details to it make a well-rounded story.

It's now time to put these sets together for one final, grand matrix. In the Grand Matrix, you'll lay down all seventy-eight cards and look at them all as one big unit.

Exercise: The Grand Matrix

When I construct a matrix, I use the floor because it's fun to get a bird's-eye perspective over the cards. If you're unable to use the whole floor, your bed or counter can provide adequate space.

If your deck is mixed and out of order, you might want to put them back into order. Which suit you put after the majors doesn't matter, but this chapter has been using an order of swords, wands, cups, and pentacles. When your deck is "in order," you can move on to making the Grand Matrix itself.

Start with making a two-column Majors Matrix. Place the Fool and the World card at the top. Then lay down cards one through ten under this. Then lay down cards eleven through twenty. Under this matrix, lay down a Minors Matrix. Place each of the court cards in the same row as their minors. Your layout should look like the following diagram:

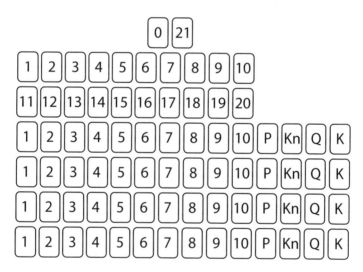

The Grand Matrix Layout

The Grand Matrix helps you investigate and unlock all the secrets of a single tarot deck. Once it's constructed, you can compare and contrast elements of the whole deck. Look at each column as if it were a single entity—what similarities and themes appear? Now do the same with each row.

Do you collect tarot decks? Try laying out multiple matrices. Lay these decks down on the floor and explore them side by side. It's amazing what patterns, themes, and ideas develop when viewing multiple decks.

Tarot is a wonderful tool with many layers. As you've seen in this first chapter, the connections begin immediately and with little knowledge. As you dive deeper into the cards, learning their meanings, and how you want to use them to enhance your life, you'll step onto a lifelong journey with your decks. They'll worm their way into many aspects of your life. And you'll grow and develop your own connections with both your decks and your usage. Tarot works because we believe in the power of the images guiding our psyche into making meaningful messages with them. It is a life-long journey to understand who we are and our place in the world.

Tarot is my daily devotional. It's my lifelong companion. I take the big, pondering questions I have and see if the cards can provide answers to them. I use the cards daily as a study guide and immediately apply the lessons in practical ways.

Tarot also provides this for me in many different ways. It gives me direction on projects I want to do, and it gives me advice on which things to do and maybe say.

Tarot is also my inner compass. It helps point me in the direction that my higher self and sense of truth wants me to go in. It gently (and sometimes not so gently) tells me things I should remove from my life. When I lay cards down, they become a step-by-step map to help me get where I want to be.

Finally, tarot is a cypher. It helps me use my experiences to decode the universe and understand what happens inside the dream. If our lives are lived as a dream, then tarot helps us decode the symbols and archetypes in our lives.

Now that you know a little bit more about my tarot philosophy, let's get you acquainted with your own deck. Ready to dive in and experiment with your cards?

For further study and reflection on the topics included in this chapter, look for the following books:

Leon, Dai. *Origins of the Tarot: Cosmic Evolution and the Principles of Immortality*. Berkeley, CA: Frog Books, 2009.

Polson, Willow. *The Veil's Edge: Exploring the Boundaries of Magic*. New York: Kensington Publishing, 2003.

Pollack, Rachel. *Tarot Wisdom: Spiritual Teachings and Deeper Meanings.* St. Paul, MN: Llewellyn Publications, 2003.

Quinn, Paul. *Tarot for Life: Reading the Cards for Everyday Guidance and Growth.* Wheaton, IL: Quest Books, 2009.

Chapter 2

Card and Spread Interpretation
Unpacking the Language of Tarot

By the end of this chapter you'll:

- Unpack the code for each card

- Learn four ways to read each card

After people discover I read tarot, I get asked one of two questions. The first is the inevitable "Ooh, can I have a reading?" after which I point them to my website, where they can order a reading. The second question, "Tell me what they mean" is the harder question for me to answer. Each card has many meanings and there's no quick way to speak about all of them.

Tarot card meanings aren't static. Each has a dynamic range of meanings from light to dark. Each book you read and each person you talk to will never give you the same exact answer. This is the art behind reading tarot. There are many ways to "read" a tarot card, as you shall see, and there is really no single correct way to read a card. Learning what the cards mean to you, their essences and range of applications, and being able to articulate how they relate to a situation are important lessons of tarot.

Let me repeat this because it is so important: There is no single correct way to read the cards! They are as diverse as you are as a person. The meaning you select at any given point in time will be the right message to say according to the conditions and factors surrounding the reading you perform. Some of these factors include the spread you're working with, the client and their question, and your mood.

Understanding Tarot Language

In some respects, studying tarot is like learning a whole new language. Just as English has its nouns, verbs, and adjectives, tarot has a structure. When you take time to learn what a card means, you are building a personal language with the cards. The exercises in this section will help you break the code in learning tarot's language. At the end of this section, you'll have a good working knowledge of what the cards can mean for you.

We'll first look at the colors in the cards and figure out what emotions they evoke. Then we'll look at the numbers and how they fit into the equation. We'll also crack the code open by picking apart the symbols on each card so you build up a whole set of meanings to work from.

I teach card meanings this way because I believe everyone should listen and honor their intuition when looking at the cards. Books filled with meanings by experts tends to become a crutch. I wish I had been taught this way when I first started out.

Using the experiences, beliefs, and knowledge you gained through your life helps you master the cards in your own voice. It also creates an authentic and powerful bond between you and your deck.

Are you ready to create your own meanings? Grab your deck, pen, and journal ... and read on.

Color

Tarot imagery is rich with color. Unless your deck of choice is black and white, I'm betting it has lots of colors. Some artists deliberately select the colors to apply to each image, which is especially true with the Rider-Waite-Smith deck where the colors adhere to a strict guideline for the Golden Dawn. The practice of magical color correspondence was common during the early days of esoteric deck design. Tarot wasn't just used for fortunes; it was used to create magic and make change happen in ourselves and the world.

Color theory suggests colors and their combinations evoke feelings in each person when they're used. We're wired to do this on an unconscious basis. For example, general cultural consensus associates red with love, anger, pain, and stop.

However, red can have other, more personal meanings to each of us. For me, red means heat (like the warmth associated with fire), anger, and general unpleasantness. On the other hand, blue is my color for love.

We start our investigation of card meanings with color, since we notice colors immediately when we lay a card down. We'll look at the cards as singular entities and compare them with other cards in their suit, and across the whole deck to look for patterns, similarities, and differences.

EXERCISE: COLOR ASSOCIATION

Pick a card, any card. Select a card at random, or you can perform this exercise as you go through the deck in order.

Look at the colors on the card. What feelings do they evoke? Do you notice subtle shifts in your mood as you continue to gaze at the card? This is the effect colors have on you.

Turn to a blank page in your journal. Write the card name and date across the top and fold the sheet lengthwise to create two columns. Write the name of the first color you noticed in the left column. Skip a few lines, then write the next color down. Continue to list colors until you've got them all.

Brainstorm as many associations as you can for each color in the right column. Do this quickly. Don't censor yourself. For an added challenge, keep a time limit of ten minutes to each card.

Don't panic if your mind draws a blank for associations. Sometimes it takes a while for you to get used to this sort of exercise. Relax and allow your subconscious mind to make connections. The faster you run this exercise, the less time your inner editor gets to derail your connections.

When you have finished the first card, do this exercise again with the rest of the deck.

For example:

The Fool from the Universal Waite deck. The main colors seem to be white, yellow, and red, so I write those down on the left side of the page. I set a timer and begin to think about those colors. White: purity, snow, cold, light, absence of darkness, glue. Yellow: the sun, sunflowers, daffodils, Kender's favorite color, summer and spring, the south, fire, corn. Red: anger, passion, chaos, roses, love, stop sign.

There are no right or wrong answers. Don't edit your responses. We're creating an associations catalog for the colors found on each card. This exercise gives us a personalized key of what each color means as it relates to each card. Use this guide to explore how the numbers might bring answers to your readings.

EXERCISE: COLOR COMPARISON

Pick cards from your deck at random. Start with two and work your way up to as many as you can handle.

Look at the cards. Stare at the colors on all the cards until they blur together and become one.

Answer these questions: How do the colors play off each card? What stories or patterns emerge? It's okay if it takes some time for associations to arise. Relax, don't over think the answers; allow your subconscious mind to make connections.

For a bigger challenge, do a Grand Matrix and compare and contract all the colors in the deck at one time. How does each suit utilize color to get emotion across?

Number

Numerology and the study of what numbers mean plays a big role in tarot meanings. You can do a whole reading based on the numbers each card has. Some readers forget to look at the patterns of numbers and how they correlate to where a seeker is in their life. Therefore, when you are learning card meanings, looking at the numbers can give you important info into your current position in the cycles of your life.

I've seen two patterns with the numbers of both the major arcana and minor arcana. The twenty-two cards of the major arcana can be divided up into sets of three. The Magician (I) through the Chariot (VII) show us a dependent relationship. Strength (VIII) to Temperance (XIV) shows how we create a separation from our dependence and learn to become independent. Finally, the Devil (XV) through the World (XXI) show a re-integration, or interdependence, allowing the parts of a system to work together in harmony to better the whole. Another familiar three-stage circuit of the majors is the idea of childhood, adulthood, and elderly stages of life.

The minor arcana also have patterns within their numbers. My favorite pattern to use takes the four stages of Stephen

Covey's *The Seven Habits of Highly Effective People*. Ace through three suggest the beginnings of a new project, or manifestation, where you are excited and ready to tackle the task at hand. Cards four through seven show how the cycle can change from excitement to frustration and depression as circumstances don't go as planned. However, the eights and nines show perseverance and the ability to overcome obstacles to make good progress. The ten releases the project and ends the cycle so you can start it all over again with a new idea.

EXERCISE: NUMBER ASSOCIATION

In this exercise, we'll look at the number on a card. As your brain takes in the number, think about what the number means to you. You can relate birthday experiences, cultural lore, or general thoughts on whether or not you like the number.

Turn to a blank page in your journal. Write the date across the top. List down the numbers from zero to twenty-two. Put a few lines in between each number.

Brainstorm any associations you have for each number. Do this quickly. Don't censor yourself. For an added challenge, set a timer for 10 minutes.

Don't panic if your mind draws a blank for associations. Sometimes it takes a bit for you to get used to this sort of exercise. Relax and allow your subconscious mind to make connections. The faster you run this exercise, the less time your inner editor gets to derail your connections.

For example:

The number four: four seasons, four walls in a room, four cardinal directions, 4-H community, four-leaf clover, the nuclear family (mother, father, daughter, son), four humors, four elements. I was four in first grade.

There are no right or wrong answers. Don't edit your responses. We're creating an associations catalog for the numbers found in your deck. You're creating a personalized key of what each number means. Use this guide to explore how the numbers might bring nuances to your readings.

Exercise: Number Comparison

Locate all the cards with the same numbers. We're going to compare and contrast how the numbers shift when associated with each suit. This exercise works great with the Grand Matrix where you look at the columns and evaluate the whole deck.

Look at the cards as a group (or columns, if you are doing the Matrix) and move your eyes over all the cards as if they were a single image.

Answer these questions in your journal. How does the number relate to each image? Are there any differences between the cards? How do the cards in the rows share numerical data? What stories or patterns emerge?

It's okay if it takes some time to build associations. Relax, don't over-think the answers; allow your subconscious mind to make connections.

For an advanced exercise, lay down all the numbers in the same suit. See how the numbers move from one to the next as you stare at the images. See if you can identify the story unfolding in the suit.

Symbol

Symbols are objects that represent an idea, another item, or a process containing meaning to the person identifying the symbol. In a way, the exercises for colors and numbers were also examining symbols on the cards. Now we'll move onto focusing our attention on the specific objects contained in each image.

Understanding the personal connection to a symbol is an important way to create strong card definitions. The exercises in this section help you to identify your card's core symbols and brainstorm ways to relate to them using your knowledge and experiences. You can use this symbol dictionary from personal experiences, dreams, or knowledge gained from reading books and watching your favorite shows.

EXERCISE: SYMBOL DICTIONARY

A few years ago, I started creating a symbol dictionary. This pocket-sized Storyboard Moleskine journal contains the name, shape, and definition of various symbols I've found, created, and used. For example, a five-pointed star has the following associations: dreams, magic, and hope for a better universe. I keep logs of symbols appearing in my world so I know what has or has not worked throughout my studies.

In this exercise, you'll work with a single card, focusing on the different symbols located on the card. Many objects appearing on each card can make reading the card easier. They become symbols you can draw meanings from. The flowers, the suit's names, people, and even the locations can trigger your mind into creating connections. Crafting a guide to your own personal connection between the symbols helps build your confidence as a reader.

Take out your tarot deck, your pen, and a journal. You're welcome to use your current journal for this study, or you can start a new book for your findings. Set up the pages by dividing them in half. Fold the pages lengthwise, or draw a line down the middle of the page. Write the symbol name (or draw it) on the left. Add your associations on the right side.

Flip the first card over on your deck. Look at the image closely. What do you see? Anything drawn on the card can be a symbol, a key to unlock the card's meaning. Feeling overwhelmed? Breathe and select the first five items that jump out at you. If the card is from the minor arcana, start with the suit item: stick for wands, chalice for cups, coin for pentacles, sword for ... well, swords. Write this symbol's name down or sketch the image.

Think about what this item means to you. If you flipped a sword over, think about what a sword is and does: Swords cut, they are weapons, they remind me of the medieval ages, and they remain my zombie weapon of choice.

Note these and all the other associations you have in your journal. Got five symbols down? Move on to another card and repeat the process. This may take some time. You don't want to do this in a single session. Recording your thoughts and definitions about symbols is worth its study and time.

EXERCISE: SYMBOL COMPARISON

Take out your tarot deck. Let's compare the cards containing similar symbols to see if their meanings change from card to card. This exercise works great with the Grand Matrix where you look at the columns.

Pick a symbol from your dictionary. Go through your deck and find all the cards where the symbol appears. Lay them out in a row. Move your eyes over each card.

Answer these questions: Do these symbols shift the card meaning if more of them appear on the cards? How does the symbol's location shed light into what it means for the card? Do the cards share symbolic data? What stories or patterns emerge?

Write down your observations. It's okay if it takes some time for associations to bubble up. Relax, don't over think the answers; allow your subconscious mind to make connections.

Alternatively, do this exercise with two or more decks. Try taking a Rider-Waite-Smith deck, Crowley's Thoth deck, and your most recent acquisition in your deck collection. Look at the same cards from the three decks. Pick out parts from the image which catch your eye. What are the symbols trying to tell you? Are similar symbols included across the decks? Do they share the same meaning or do they have different messages? Do the different symbols on the cards affect the overall meaning of the card?

Write down your observations. Isolate the differences and tease out what you think they're trying to say.

For example, the Shadowscapes Tarot added black swans to its Five of Swords. What does their addition tell you? How does this compare to a standard tarot deck's Five of Swords?

Recognizing the symbols in your deck and understanding how you relate to the cards helps connect you to the deck in a strong way. Doing these exercises helps you learn as you walk through the cards and as you weave a reading for your clients. Interpreting cards this way shows you the infinite possibilities of meanings the cards can have as they change from person to person.

Keywords

A keyword is a single word trigger that helps you unlock one of the meanings contained within the card. Assigning a single word to each card is another quick and easy method to build your tarot vocabulary. There are many ways to build one-word associations with each tarot card's imagery. In this section I'll share two exercises that will teach you how.

Exercise: Flashcard Keyword Game

This exercise is an intuitive game you can do alone or with friends. Break out your cards and turn one over. Take a short glance at the card, then say one word to represent what you see. This word should be the first association that pops into your head. Don't think about it. Act on instinct, don't take longer than five seconds. If you spend more time, then you're allowing the rational left-brain to interfere with your intuition. Let your gut do the work.

The trick is to act on instinct. Don't look at the card for too long. Say what comes into your mind. Don't attach judgment to the word.

If you're alone, write the word down in your journal and move on to the next card. Your goal is to get a single word down for all seventy-eight cards in the least amount of time possible.

For example:

Three of Swords—heartbreak. Written down due to the unforgettable symbol of a heart pierced with three swords plunged downward.

Flash card exercises help prime the pump when you're getting ready to read for others. Tarot cards will always evoke emotion and impressions. I've never met a tarot reader who didn't get drawn into—or repulsed by—the various imagery. Doing this exercise shows how quickly and intuitively you can build a single card definition for each card.

When you have a keyword for each one, you can then place the cards into categories: positive and negative. You'll also use these meanings as the start of a fully-fledged reading for others. Many authors have written full books exploring the various shades of card meanings.

EXERCISE: REAL-WORLD APPLICATION GAME

In this exercise, you'll adapt keywords to real-world situations and problems. Get your friends together and have them join in on the fun. You'll end up getting multiple suggestions for the same situation.

Try coming up with keywords to the following situations:

- Relationships: dating, marriage, coworkers.

- Money

- Career

- Spirituality

- Health

As with all the other exercises thus far, don't censor yourself. Later, review all the ideas you have in your journal, especially the silly and weird ones. Sometimes, the weirder the connection, the deeper and more original the idea is.

Going through this exercise teaches you how to apply the meanings and symbols to any possible category potential clients may toss your way. Reading tarot requires flexibility to apply seventy-eight cards to a person's question.

Quotes

I'm fond of quotes; they are powerful reminders of what we can accomplish. You can find quotes almost anywhere—from books to online quote resources to tea bags. Surprisingly, keeping a collection of quotes can also aid in unlocking tarot card meanings.

A few years ago, I participated in a year-long deck study group. We used Ciro Marcetti's Legacy of the Divine Tarot, and our weekly get-togethers focused on learning about the cards. I noticed over the year that some of the group used the deck's book. Each card contained a quote, and for those people, examining each quote helped members get to their a-ha moments. These quotes seemed to poignantly capture the atmosphere, vibe, and flavor of Ciro's masterful art. They became a strong meaning for the card.

When it came to creating workshops to share our knowledge with others, these quotes became an integral part of our lessons. We integrated the quotes into the workshops, sometimes using them to frame the material we shared. We also used them to give attendees food for thought as they constructed their own meanings.

I suggest you collect quotes during your study sessions. Pull them from a wide range of sources: your favorite books, movies, famous people, other tarot books, or online. As you read and study, these quotes can help illustrate your passion and how you interpret the events in your life.

Keeping quotes to best illustrate important aspects of tarot study and each individual card can broaden your horizon. Every time you think of the quote, you'll unconsciously tap into the power of the card as well. If you ever get stuck doing readings for yourself, or for others, recall or use the quote as a jumping off point to continue the session.

Four Ways to Read a Card

You've unlocked kernels of meaning from within each tarot card, so now it's time to dive a bit deeper and learn how to apply those meanings in readings. Synthesizing all the parts of the card into something meaningful is the next step in learning the language of tarot.

As I see it, there are four ways to read a card: symbolic, experience, storytelling, and psychic. Each way has its purposes, strengths, and weaknesses. Use these techniques as a template to uncover your own personal style. If one or many of these styles don't tickle your fancy, that's okay. Each reader develops their strengths.

Symbolic Readings

A symbolic reading focuses on the meanings and connections from the symbols in the images. Remember, everything on a card is a symbol used to answer a client's question. Look at what stands out to you, describe them in terms of how they relate to the question at hand. Refer to your symbol, number, and color dictionaries to create deeper references.

For example:

Auburn has a new boyfriend; she wants to know if he's the one. The cards get shuffled and out comes the Lovers. Scanning the card reveals a lot of red and purple colors. We talk about the colors, how red is a color of love, and how it can be a warning sign. But the purple on the card suggests a spiritual connection. The number of the card, six, connects this card to the heart chakra, and is in the middle of a cycle. We talk about how the relationship is going, and she tells me it's going a bit faster than she wants. We discuss ways to slow the relationship down so Auburn can accurately tell if he's the one for her. She leaves with homework on how to communicate with this partner.

How would you read the Lovers in a new relationship reading? It's okay to come up with ideas and a path different from mine. Remember, there is no wrong way to read a card.

Experience Readings

Everyone on this planet lives a unique life. Our personalities, youth, schooling, and relationships give us a distinctive eye on life and a long list of experiences. When you read tarot, you are allowed to draw upon these experiences to act as a guide or allegory for yourself or clients on how to act next.

Sometimes when I read for others, I'll tell clients what the cards mean by using an illustrated example from my own life. It's relatable and shows my clients how their issues can also affect others. Not only do they know where others have been, they also receive wisdom gained from another who has gone through a similar experience. Of course, it's up to them to decide what to do with the information; sometimes nothing trumps experience.

Storytelling Readings

Tarot tells a tale. Each and every card has one. In a reading, the answer becomes the story, spilled across several cards. Take a deep breath and look for the story the cards suggest. Let the images become scenes that inspire you, the storyteller, to speak. Start with "once upon a time …" and let the people or creatures on the card talk. Describe an event. What is going on? Be creative, figure out what happened before or after the card came into being. What might happen if the image on the card does come true?

Telling a story is a great way to read the cards, especially if you feel blocked or aren't sure what the cards are saying to you. The storytelling technique is also useful if you're not sure what the card means in the position of the spread. When you are faced with one of these situations, just take a deep breath, close your eyes, and allow the story to unfold naturally.

Psychic Readings

The final method is psychic readings. We are born with various intuitive gifts. You know those hunches or flashes of weird insight you get? These are psychic gifts at work. Whether you believe these messages are God tapping into your mind, a spirit guide watching over you, or coincidence, these insights can be invaluable during a reading.

I once had a client who inquired about her health. Tarot is a wonderful tool, and while you can gain insight into all aspects of your life, I don't see the cards as a replacement for the advice of trained professionals. I am not licensed to practice medicine, psychology, or law. I always let clients know tarot is not a replacement for a diagnosis and ask them to visit their qualified professionals first. Those professionals spent years learning and being tested in their areas of study, and no matter how psychic we can be, I firmly believe we as tarot readers are not qualified (or in some cases, certified) to provide guidance on such matters. Of course as I say this, there is a growing body of doctors, psychologists, and lawyers who have an interest in tarot. Some may even integrate the cards into their professional practices, but this is rare—not the norm. If you think of yourself as a psychic and offer readings of this type, be aware of the laws regarding answering health, financial, or legal questions. Arm yourself with your local laws and protect yourself.

Thankfully in my client's case, she had already seen a doctor and was looking for advice on how to deal with her situation. I shuffled the cards, flipped them over, and got the High Priestess. I must have had "the look" on my face because my client reassured me how she wanted to know. What came out of my mouth astonished us both. I asked her if she had ovarian cancer. She nodded, and her husband gripped her shoulder. She asked me how I knew, and all I could say was that it came to me. Looking back, I can see the logic trail for the answer. The High Priestess is deeply connected to the feminine, and my mind made the connection to the reproductive system. However, I do believe my insight was guided by something other than experience, and that's the power of psychic intuition at work.

For further study and reflection on the topics included in this chapter, look for the following books:

Cynova, Melissa. *Kitchen Table Tarot: Pull Up a Chair, Shuffle the Cards, and Let's Talk Tarot.* Woodbury, MN: Llewellyn Publications, 2017.

Greer, Mary K. *Tarot for Your Self.* Van Nuys, CA: Newcastle Publishing Company, 1987.

Huggens, Kim. *Tarot 101: Mastering the Art of Reading the Cards.* Woodbury, MN: Llewellyn Publications, 2010.

Katz, Marcus. *Tarosophy: Tarot to Engage Life, Not Escape It.* Chaing Mai, Thailand: Salamander and Sons, 2011.

Sim, Valerie. *Tarot Outside the Box.* St. Paul, MN: Llewellyn Publications, 2004.

Chapter 3

Wide World of Spreads
Laying Cards in Intricate Patterns

By the end of this chapter you'll:

- Discover tarot spreads

- Learn about reading the cards in spreads

- Create your own tarot spreads

Tarot Spreads

Knowing card meanings is just one part of reading tarot. The second half of the equation is how you lay the cards down and use them to answer questions. Tarot spreads are the patterns you set cards into to form answers to questions you ask. Some spreads answer a single question, while others discuss a wide range of areas in your life. Spreads clarify and unlock the card messages when we need to know specific information.

Spreads guide us through what is going on rather than stringing together a hit-or-miss storyline picked off cards haphazardly on a table. Each card in a spread becomes a single snippet of information. These positions give structure to a reading that guides the answer to the surface. This is important because it helps clients understand where their reading is going and how all the symbols fit into answering their burning question. When woven together, the positions give a complete answer to the question at hand.

When people first start out, they believe the physical deck is all they'll need to start performing accurate readings—it's what I did when I bought my first deck! I stayed away from spreads because many of them, like the Celtic Cross, didn't make sense to me. I read about spreads taking hours or more to set up and then countless more hours to figure out what the cards meant and how they all related to one another. Who has time for *that*? I travel light, so the idea of needing to know massive amounts of spreads felt like I'd have to carry heavy books everywhere I went. All I wanted was to be prepared when someone asked me to read for them … or so I thought.

I attended the 2011 Reader's Studio in New York where Barbara Moore talked about tarot spreads. It revised the way I felt about using spreads. Her class showed me I was missing one important ingredient to a well-rounded reading: using a good spread helps focus the reading and gives new perspectives regarding the question we may not have considered.

I believe readers should have a basic knowledge of spreads. In my own practice, I employ custom on-the-fly and pre-made spreads. Creating spreads allows us to be flexible and can deliver powerful specific answers for clients with unique questions. For generic and repetitive questions, I keep a short but well-rounded stack of spreads in my tool kit that are perfect for any occasion.

Types of Spreads

As I mentioned earlier, there are two categories of spreads: pre-made and self-created.

Pre-made spreads are layouts found in books, websites, and from other readers who are willing to share with you. These patterns have been created for a specific purpose or are general patterns you can use to get answers. Collecting spreads can be just as addictive as collecting decks. There are so many out there and each has their own unique voice and insight. Search the web and see what I mean.

Self-created spreads are ones you craft. They take creativity and ingenuity to design. What happens when you make your own spreads?

- Your readings become more alive and vibrant and true.

- They reflect your personality, honoring both you and your client.

Before you can learn to design your own spreads, you first need to learn and experience the process behind using them, a process that includes shuffling the cards, casting the spread, and reading the cards. These are the parts to performing a reading for yourself or for others.

Shuffling Cards

Shuffling the cards is an important step before laying down cards and reading them. Mixing the cards gives you space to organize your thoughts. I take this time to focus on the client's energy if reading for one, or on the question I want answered.

I have seen people carefully shuffle a deck using one corner of the deck. Others mix the cards up as if they are playing a round of Go Fish and select cards from the pile to read from. Personally, I'm a riffler. I take the deck and split them approximately in half, then place my thumbs on the edges of one side of the card and the fingers on the other. Next, I gently bend the cards down a bit, then relax and release my thumbs so the cards on either side mix together. If you get good at this, you can then bridge the cards up so they are in a neat stack, and ready to be shuffled again. There's something relaxing about shuffling cards; the sound can be hypnotizing.

Deck size is important to shuffling. Most decks are larger than standard-sized playing cards and can be hard to work with. Practice shuffling your deck to familiarize yourself with the size of the cards and how you want to handle them. If you have small hands, sometimes turning the deck on the wide side helps when shuffling oversized cards. Practice and experiment with shuffling techniques to figure out what method works best for you and your deck.

Casting the Spread

Casting the spread, or putting cards down on the table, happens after you shuffle the cards. Many spreads include diagrams which show where to drop a card into the pattern. So, in a five card spread, you look at the diagram and lay the first card down in the first position and continue until you have put all the cards down.

For example, if I were to lay cards down for a Past, Present, and Future spread, it might look like:

The Past, Present, Future Layout

Card one is the past position. The second shows the present, and the third is the future. Each position's name colors how the card gets interpreted. Sometimes, a position reveals the positive traits of the card, while others draw out the negative aspects. When using pre-made spreads, the creator usually includes a descriptive position name and some text on what the spread means. The description is often a question the position needs to answer. Many, but not all, also include a spread diagram so you know what design to set the cards in.

Reading Cards in a Spread

After the cards are in position, it's time to decipher the cards in relation to those positions. There are many ways to perform an actual reading. This is how I work on my stories; your readings may be different. I start by talking about the each card's number and elemental energy. This helps me prime the pump for the amazing and creative information that comes through as I speak. I then talk about the story as I see it. Finally, I relate each card back to its position and reinforce how it relates to the question.

For example, let's say Jennifer comes to me for a three-card Past, Present, and Future reading. She just wants to know what's going on around her. I shuffle my deck and lay the cards down.

The first card gets flipped over and we see the Emperor. I take some time to look at the card and let all the information I know about the card flood into my mind. When I am ready, I tell Jennifer about how the Emperor is a card of boundaries and rules. He is the father archetype. She looks back at me and says she's not into structure and boundaries. This gives me the impression she may be missing the lesson this card teaches. As this card falls in a past position, I tell her she had to recently lay down the law and give her family some rules and structure. Perhaps she had to do this for herself in order to create the space she needed to move forward with her projects in her life.

I turn over the next card, the King of Pentacles. It shows a man sitting on his throne in a lush garden. I begin by saying how stable this personality is. He is a fair ruler, and all his subjects come to hear what he has to say. He is a fixed position in their lives, trustworthy and just. As this card falls in the present position, I relate this card to the present position. I tell Jennifer how redefining her boundaries has given her the power to become a real leader, someone others can depend on. This stability allows her the freedom to understand what is going on in her life and will push her into the future feeling strong and confident.

Finally, I reveal the 10 of Cups in the future position. This card shows a happy family enjoying a picturesque sunny day. Children are playing as the adoring couple looks on. A rainbow blooms in the sky. I tell Jennifer how this card heralds a time of happiness and prosperity. With stability comes opportunities to bring in all the good life offers.

When you read cards, you are mostly focused on what cards appear in the spread. Sometimes looking at what doesn't appear in readings can give valuable insight. In the above reading, for example, there are no wands or swords. This tells me Jennifer is a smart, active individual and she doesn't have to worry about what is going on in her mind. The biggest focus for her reading is bringing balance and stability into her life to attain her dreams.

Creating Tarot Spreads

There are numerous ways to create a spread. In this section are five steps to designing your own spreads. In a nutshell these are: identify the purpose, get specific, pick the right number of cards, figure out the card pattern, and experiment.

Follow your intuition when designing your own spreads; it will guide you into discovering what's right or wrong. By following these guidelines, your spreads become meaningful and powerful. When you share them with others and they're used successfully, your spreads gain strength.

In this section I'll create an on-the-spot spread using these steps.

Identify the Purpose

Identifying the purpose of the spread is the first step in designing your own spread. Brainstorming is a great way to generate spread ideas. What topics interest you? What challenges are you facing in your life? What goals do you want to achieve? Tarot can be a wonderful problem-solving tool.

Listen to your intuition. It knows what desires and questions you have. Allow it to help you sort out categories for spreads. Talk to your friends. What issues are they facing? How do they help you when you approach them with questions? Knowing how they walk you through a problem can bring amazing insights to use as positions in a spread.

What topic or question will your spread address? What is the focus? Sometimes the focus isn't the question, it's the idea behind the question.

In creating a sample spread for this section, I asked a friend of mine what challenges she faced at the moment. She told me her family was looking for a new house. Using the brainstorming method (and adding in the experience of having moved from one place to another recently), I came up with the following list of possible factors: new house, location importance, family considerations, children, pets, proximity to school/work/ amenities, and cost.

All of these factors combine into defining a spread's purpose and can be used for creating a great spread. This step doesn't have to take a long time; it took me no more than five minutes to generate this small list. As you work through it, resist the urge to censor ideas. Write everything down, even if it arises more than once.

Get Specific
The next step in this process is to take your brainstorm and hone the ideas into priorities. There are many directions and possibilities a reading can go no matter what the topic might be. In this step, pick and blend which bits of information to include. The key point here is to be specific. Generic spreads seem disjointed and can lose focus quickly. Instead, look at the core issue or question you are trying to understand and break it down into components. Your topic may have a lot of components that need to be addressed in order to come up with a holistic answer. If this happens, and you don't want your spread to be too complex, you can divide the information up into more than one spread.

In our sample spread, the general idea tossed at me was "help me find a new house." I came up with the following list: new house, location importance, family considerations, children, pets, proximity to school/work/amenities, and cost.

Our sample spread shows some signs of specificity, yet I want to go deeper to understand what "getting a new house" means. I grab a pen and paper, write down each item on the left, and start posing more questions to add depth.

New House: Are we talking a new place or older home? Is this to rent or buy? How many rooms? Does room count matter? Large backyard? Gas or electric heating?

Location: City limits or out in the country? Homeowners' association dues? Is the home already in the established school boundaries for the kids?

Children/Pets: What do the kids think of moving? How will moving during a school year affect their situation?

Cost: Mortgage/rent costs? How will the new place affect their financial state? How much upkeep will the house require? Can they have a house and save for the future?

See how detailed this step can get? It took me no more than five minutes to generate these additional questions. You can take longer, but beware of getting stuck down the rabbit hole. Because I'm designing this spread for someone in particular, she gets final say on the depth.

After receiving the feedback, we decide on the following arrangement. The resulting spread is more focused and specific than the brainstorm session.

Card One: General moving thoughts. How do you feel about moving?

Card Two: Location considerations. Does it matter where we move to?

Card Three: Family's emotions. What emotions does each family member have about this move? (One card is drawn for each member)

Card Four: Cost considerations. How does moving impact our finances?

Card Five: Outcome. Knowing the four factors, how will the move go?

As you can see, these positions came out of getting specific. They're open ended enough to allow the cards to answer in their own way without duplicating information. In addition, cards can get added or removed based on what details get revealed.

Pick the Right Number of Cards

In this step, we choose the number of cards your spread will contain. How many cards (or decks, for that matter) your spreads will have is all up to you. From my experience, the more cards a spread has, the less time you can spend on each individual card and how it relates to the original question. Time is important. Clients don't want you to spend hours on answering their question.

In fact, I budget my time out for all my readings. I don't use more than four cards for a half-hour session, and I don't go over six cards in an hour. I make sure I have enough time in my sessions to dive as deeply into each card as we can. Of course, other readers have their own preferences. It's up to you to decide your own personal limitations and how you can deliver the best reading for your clients without taking up too much time.

In our house-hunting spread example, we had seven buckets. Those seven topics generated a lot of questions and additional bits of information. After communicating with my friend, we settled on five positions. Since one of the positions includes drawing a card for each family member (there are five others in the family), this bumps the spread up to nine total cards. While this goes against my general personal desire for a six-card maximum, we felt it was important to know each family member's thoughts.

Card Pattern Science

Spread imagery design is important. The sequence in which you place down cards matters. In this step of spread creation we play with patterns, designs, and images. How does the design of your spread affect the flow of information? Does lining up cards in a horizontal row have the same impact as a vertical one? What about a circular design?

Developing your spread patterns is the fun part. This is when you get to lay down cards and use the power of sight to add insight into a reading. Will you make a circle, star, cross, or triangle? Only you can decide.

In the house hunting spread, we have five positions with one position expanding to five extra cards—one for each family member.

Card One: General moving thoughts. How do you feel about moving?

Card Two: Location considerations. Does it matter where we move to?

Card Three: Family's emotions. What emotions does each family member have about this move? (Draw one card for each member and pet in the family)

Card Four: Cost considerations. How will this move impact our finances?

Card Five: Outcome. Knowing the four factors, how will the move go?

Looking at the spread so far, I wanted to craft the spread in the shape of a house. Breaking down the house, this meant I needed to lay cards down in a box and a triangle. I took out a tarot deck and began playing around with shapes.

- Outcome as chimney

- Location and cost as roof

- Family members as the external structure. I toyed with the idea of putting everyone on the same plane but then I put the parents as the side walls and then the rest of the family as the floor.

In the end, I settled on the following pattern:

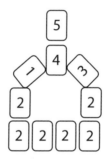

The House Buying Layout

The rationale for each card is as follows:

Outcome on top (card 5). The outcome is the most important piece of information, while it is the last card to be drawn from the deck I place it on top because outcomes sway decisions.

Location and cost as a roof (cards 2 and 4). These two bits of information are important because they affect all aspects of the family. The location is important for school and work commutes. The cost is important because it affects family spending and savings.

Originally, I wanted all the family members on the same level but this family has six members and not every family member is equal. The parents make decisions and the rest of the family must live with it. Therefore, the parents become the walls, and everyone else forms the floor.

With a layout locked in, we moved onto the final step.

Experimenting Phase

The last step in this spread creation process is to use and test out your spreads. Test them out by using the spread. Make sure the questions and spread design do what you want them to accomplish. Share your spreads with a few friends and find out how their experiences went. Sometimes you'll have a great spread idea but when you put it into practice, the spread doesn't work. Maybe the shape doesn't make sense or the positions give the wrong feedback. The point is, you'll never know how the spread holds up unless you put it into use and get feedback.

With our completed New House spread, it was time for me to try it out. I could just do this spread for my friend and let it speak for itself, but if this spread was going to be consistent and usable, more data points were needed. So I grabbed a deck, shuffled the cards with the intention of helping imaginary families find their house, and proceeded with some test readings. Once I was confident the spread worked, I then did the spread for real and shared it and the results with my friend.

I also spent some time to tweak it a bit more to make it less specific for this one family and more generic for others. For example, I figured I could add other factors to this move such as public transit, amenities, or even friendship thoughts as either the walls or the floor bits to this house diagram.

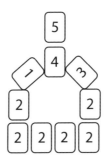

The House Buying Layout

Why bother tweaking the spread after the use has been complete? Spreads have a life of their own. In order to be practical, useful, and insightful, spreads must be worked with and tweaked.

In fact, one of my work-horse spreads has gone through its third revision. In the beginning, this spread used five cards. However, working with the spread over the years, I've gained insight into how it works. I've clarified the intent and goals, and as a result, the number of cards and their meanings changed. It now uses four cards and acts more like a recipe for setting plans in motion than a spread to reveal information. With each iteration, the spirit and resourcefulness of this spread get honed and refined every time. It also shows me the power of a good spread and how it can be strengthened to inspire lives of others.

Practice, Practice, Practice

Studying tarot is a life-long journey. When you think you may have discovered "the ultimate answer to life, the universe, and everything" (besides the number forty-two) the cards slap you upside the head and reveal something new. These discoveries remind me just how far I am from understanding how the universe works. Revelations happen, and they happen often.

After you've exhausted your own personal knowledge, start studying from others. Take the money you worked hard to save up and buy tarot books, indulge in classes, or meet up with others who have the same passion as you do. Explore the world of tarot and those who spend a lot of their time with it.

Practice your skills as a reader, especially if you are serious about going professional. Doing readings for others builds your confidence with the cards and teaches you what spreads work best for any given situation. Reading for others is a unique beast in its own right, and there is no real formula on how it is done—just jump right in and find out what your client needs. Take a deep breath, shuffle the cards, and start interpreting. As you read for others and practice, you'll uncover what type of reader you are. Your reading style will evolve over the years as you continue playing with the cards (I know mine has) and learning new techniques. Don't be afraid to test out new ideas with others; it'll make you stronger.

Reading cards for others also helps you understand the cards better. Each question brings out card nuances. Sometimes your clients will point out details on your cards you may never have seen before. They may also treat you with some new insights. Once you learn tarot, you will never stop uncovering new insights about the cards or techniques.

Using the cards in various ways helps you builds knowledge and repertoire. See how the cards can fit into your current hobbies and passions. It'll help you bond with your deck and give you creative connections. I am proof that this is possible—this has been my path and journey for many years.

The remainder of this book is going to stretch your tarot-based knowledge. You'll learn new ways of incorporating tarot cards and tarot meanings in your life. You'll find a writing voice with the cards. You'll even undergo powerful transformations as you learn with the cards, adding archetypes in meditation and in ritual. Are you ready?

For further study and reflection on the topics included in this chapter, look for the following books:

Fiorini, Jeanne. *Tarot Spreads & Layouts: A User's Manual for Beginning and Intermediate Readers.* Atglen, PA: Schiffer Publishing, 2010.

Michelsen, Teresa. *Designing Your Own Tarot Spreads.* St. Paul, MN: Llewellyn Publications, 2003.

Moore, Barbara. *Tarot Spreads: Layouts & Techniques to Empower Your Readings.* Woodbury, MN: Llewellyn Publications, 2012.

Part 2
What You Can Do with Tarot

Chapter 4

Daily Writing Practices

Daily Deck Interactions

By the end of this chapter you'll:

- Use tarot as a journaling companion

- Create a tarot Personal Data Assistant (PDA)

- Keep a history of your tarot journey
  with your tarot PDA

Intro to Journaling

Journaling is a writing technique which allows us to express our thoughts on paper. Journals keep notes, lists, and information in one place so they aren't forgotten. Combined with a tarot practice, journaling helps us see patterns in the cards as we draw them over time. There are many kinds of journals you can keep. This chapter covers a few systems.

Journaling is an awesome way to dialog with the cards and leave a record of your own personal thoughts. Your journal can be as private as you need it to be. You don't have to share what you've put on paper unless you want to. Many tarot enthusiasts including myself record thoughts about the cards and readings. In fact, I have several different tarot journals: one includes card thoughts and quotes, another records readings I've done for reflection and further study, and I also keep a daily log of cards drawn.

Journaling Ground Rules

Before I start a journal of any type, I set down some rules. These help remind me what I'm tracking and keep me grounded.

Keep your hand moving. The inner editor inside your brain is strong. If you don't keep your hand moving, that critical voice has the tendency to butt in and mock what you do. Moving your pen (or your fingers across the keyboard) gives your creative muscles the freedom needed to get your thoughts out as fast as possible. As we say in the writing world, "messy first drafts required." If you need to transfer the data you've uncovered into a separate book, do it afterward. Duplicating also helps you recall the data later on. As for me, I keep much of my tarot information on my computer, something that will be addressed later in this chapter.

Date every entry. Your journals are written records of what you've learned throughout your tarot studies. Dating entries marks your progress against time's passage. It measures your academic work. When you have a date, you can look back and pinpoint the exact moment when key knowledge became part of your daily habit. Keeping digital records? Date each file—actually type the date into your file.

There are no wrong answers. Tarot study is deeply personal. The symbols and images evoke different feelings and memories for each person. What you think a card means is *never* inferior to what you read in a book. No two readers are alike, and everyone thinks differently. Trust your intuition and gut reactions, and write everything down. You can also change your mind later, but what's important is keeping a document when you had a particular thought.

Be easy on yourself. Don't let the inner editor get to you. Learning the cards isn't easy. Even I get stuck sometimes. When you get frustrated or your mind goes blank, take a deep breath. Still your mind until something bubbles up. If I'm reading for others, I might allow them to lend their input as to what the message might be.

Play with color. Expand your entries by playing with colored pens. Gone are the days of using black and blue. Keep track of different aspects of your study using color.

Black can denote shadow work; blue for dreams; green for spell and ritual observations. Try using red when you add to previous entries. I have a friend who uses colors in her journals and even keeps a handy index of color meanings. Did I mention how fun using different colors can be?

Above all, have fun. This last rule is also the most important. As with any activity in life, studying tarot and keeping a journal are meant to be fun. Do new and exciting activities to help you enjoy these disciplines. Experiment with your writing style, doodle in your books, learn to recognize and honor your inner voice—your journals will become an extension of you. Who knows, perhaps your books will help others on their path one day.

The Importance of Recording Knowledge

Western cultures standardize education. Instructors assign tasks and tests for students who then have to prove how well they absorbed the knowledge. Tests and tasks become metrics that track the extent to which one learns a subject. Done daily, your journal entries become metrics for you to track your progress. These books become a guide and tutor through the art of reflection. By keeping records of where you were when you first started and each reading you've done, you can see the nuances in how your journey progresses. The paths we take in learning tarot techniques vary from person to person, and each record becomes a way station on the road map. When you study a new subject on your own, you become both student and teacher; your records help define the course of your instruction and also become a way to reflect on where you have been.

Here's a list of items you may want to track:

- Card meanings

- Reading styles

- Spreads you created and their evolution

My journals are records of where I have been, and they help create containers for where I want to go next. They inspire my tarot blog and podcast, and shape the nature of classes I want to teach. When I reflect on past entries, I see a path of lessons, research, and study spanning decades.

I've been keeping irregular tarot journals since I got my first deck, first as a way to record readings. I tracked spreads, the card positions, and each card's meanings for the questions I asked. I even tracked the readers if I received readings from others. All those notes expanded into keeping track of what I thought the cards meant and what their symbols were. The more I wrote, the more I understood why I needed to keep track of it all. Something important was going on: keeping clear records of all you do with tarot gives you a solid foundation for being a well-grounded and flexible tarot reader.

Journaling with Tarot

Let's start building your journal practice. The exercises in this section are gentle enough guides into the process. I've used them in my own personal practice and in the classes I teach. Give them a shot and see what comes from trying them out.

Exercise: Daily Draw

The most common practice is pulling a single card every day, which can be done in the morning or the evening. Shuffle your deck, draw a card, and jot down some thoughts on how it'll affect your day. I do my draws in the morning to see what message the cards have for me. Then I go about my day not giving it much thought. Just before bedtime, I'll revisit the message and add more information on how the card affected or influenced my day.

For your daily draw exercise, I want you to pull a card in the morning and see what information it has for your day. You're building a new habit, so pick a convenient and consistent time. Stick with this practice for one month. You'll build stamina.

If it helps, create an air of ritual when you select your card. Make sure you're in a quiet location, where you can be undisturbed. Light a candle. Say a few words. When you're ready, shuffle your deck and make the draw. Breathe. Look at the imagery. What symbols stand out? What message does the card have? Record any impressions you may have and then go about your day.

Later, before you go to bed, pull out your journal and revisit what you wrote. Use your colored pen for reflections, if you selected one. Read what you wrote in the morning. Think back to earlier: did the card change the way you went about your day? Write about how it came to play in your day. You can also add any new impressions. If you can connect the card back to a specific moment, do so. Let your imagination guide you into the cards and place yourself in the imagery.

For example:

Tuesday, I drew the Knight of Cups. When I went to record this information in my daily draw journal, I wrote down the date and the name along with: "Spent most of today steeped in my imagination. Worked on tarot book and used the creative powers to put pen to paper, just as the Knight of Cups uses his feelings and imagination to attain his quest." Sometimes your entries are short and simple. Other times you'll write lengthy notes on how the card intersected throughout your day.

EXERCISE: LIKE AND DISLIKE

Take your deck out and look at the images. You're going to go through each card as fast as you can. As you look at the image, let your intuition tell you whether or not you like or dislike the card. Move quickly and don't wake your inner editor! Trust your gut to push the card into the right stack.

When you've gone through the whole deck, pick up the like pile. We're going to figure out why you put it into the pack.

Was it the colors? The scene? The overall vibe? Write all the positive discoveries in your journal. Move onto the next card. When you're done, move onto the dislike chunk.

Want to kick this up a notch? Place a like card next to a dislike card. Compare and contrast the two cards. Where do they balance?

For example:

From the Haindl Tarot: *my* favorite card in this deck is Death. The artist drew a lovely image of a crow, a leaf that looks like it has been pressed between two pages of a book, and a skeletal hand holding a scythe coming out from a barren ground. To me, this card represents a more natural image of death and the cycles of transformation than a "pale rider on a dark horse." Crows have long been associated with death and the passage of change, and the colors in this card just appeal to me.

Conversely, the Mother of Wands in the East, who is Kali, disturbs me. I purchased this deck while I was in high school, long before I knew anything about the goddess herself. I never quite liked her attitude and image. One day while looking closely at this card to try and figure out just what exactly I didn't like, I realized that she was having sex with a dead man. Subconsciously, this triggered and put me off this card.

So from here, I could continue the journal entry on the Kali card and talk about my feelings and relationship toward sex. I could also write about how sex is a transforming ritual for our culture to turn adolescents into adults, but I think this is enough to show you how this exercise works.

Exercise: Entering the Card

Tarot card images depict complete worlds. In this exercise, you'll push beyond the borders to see what else might exist. Pull a card from your deck. Pretend it's a doorway to another world. Stare at the card's scene until a feeling or thought emerges. Let your mind wander until it snags on an idea. It's okay if it's not related to the card itself. Glance at the card until your mind comes up with a thought. The moment something stirs in your head, grab your journal and start writing it down.

This type of writing is sort of akin to automatic writing where you just allow the words and your mind to flow and you are keeping your consciousness out from editing or censoring the thoughts that get put on the page.

For example:

Science Tarot: The Hanged Man (potential energy).

This card shows a desolate landscape, almost like a plateau in the Sahara desert with some shrubs and a single Joshua tree in the background. A cliff appears to the left of me and the right side of the card dives down to another cliff. Clouds obscure my view. Standing in front of me is a huge rock formation that seems to defy all laws of physics. A cone rises up from the dirt. It holds the rock perfectly balanced. I reach out with my hand and trace the inscription on the base, $E = U$. I never took physics, so I make a note to search out what this means. The sun sets. I look to my left and see a shadow cast against the cliff wall. Instead of the cone and rock, I see the outline of a man. The air smells dry and stale and the only sound I hear is the cawing of a bird who has just landed on the stone.

Advanced Techniques

Having fun with your journal? Hungry for new techniques to try out? Well, let's kick this practice up a notch. These exercises push your creativity a bit more, use multiple cards, and will help expand your journaling prowess.

EXERCISE: REACH FOR THE STARS

Tarot is especially good at dream manifestation; my private practice is built around helping clients achieve their goals. Journaling our desires and recording the journey we took to manifestation is a wonderful way to savor the process. This exercise works best if you have a goal you'd like to achieve.

Shuffle your deck and draw two cards. Examine their images. What stands out to you? How do they answer the following questions:

– What aspect of your goal is being represented?
– What advice for attaining your dreams do they offer?
– Write the answers in your journal.

For example:

I drew the Five of Wands and the Five of Swords from the Shadowscapes Tarot. Immediately, I'm drawn to the double fives. Fives are challenging numbers in the tarot cycle. Looking at the Five of Wands, I notice the foxes and how they mirror my scattered brain. I'm so close to my dreams of getting this book done, yet the distractions, excuses, and paid work snap my attention away from getting what I want. In contrast, the Five of Swords shows no confusion. There's a laser-like focus as the angel on the card smoothly hovers forward. As an interesting side bonus, the sword bearer holds his weapon with the point towards the left, as if its ready to cut right through the silly chaos and confusion the foxes on the Five of Wands have created.

The advice these cards give me is blunt: Hunker down. Just get it done. Push on through and get the draft done.

Exercise: Inside Advice

This exercise teaches you how to use your intuitive voice. You'll need a question for this exercise. Some good examples are, "What do I need to know today?" or "What role am I supposed to be playing in this universe?" Focus on your question as you shuffle the cards. When you are ready, draw one. Look at the image and record the answer in your journal. The answer can be simple, or it can open up complex contemplation for further examination.

For example:

It's allergy season and Tom's been having flare-ups. He pulls out his deck and asks, "What do I need to know about my health?" Death appears. As a card of transformation and change, he realizes he needs to relax and know this is part of his transformation from one season to the next. This season will pass and his allergies will also pass. Death tells him that his health is in a state of transformation and he just needs to be able to ride it out … and be aware of the pollen count.

EXERCISE: REVIEW THIS

This exercise requires you to pick a book, movie, or a favorite restaurant. You're going to use tarot to craft a report on the item. Shuffle your deck and draw three cards. The first card represents what you liked. The second represents what you disliked. The final card provides you with a completely new perspective on the topic; perhaps you wouldn't have noticed or realized it on your own.

When you've figured out the message each card has, pull out your journal and start working on a draft.

For example:

While sitting at her favorite ice cream parlor, Anna drew the Two of Wands, the Knight of Swords, and the Ten of Wands. The Two of Wands reminds her of the coolness of the atmosphere, a place she can go to write and work on her projects without worry. The Knight of Swords represents the turn-over of people that come in and out of the place. It's a popular location and sometimes spending time isn't possible. The Ten of Wands provides her the perspective of having a place to go to when the work is done. She loves the richness of the ice cream and sees it as a perfect treat. Anna then uses these cards to formulate a review of the place, its atmosphere, and the food based on the cards she has drawn.

EXERCISE: REWRITING MEMORIES

Life has its ups and downs, and we have all lived through rough experiences. What if I told you there was a way to rewrite those painful moments so they affect you less? Would you be willing to try? This exercise allows you to replace those negative feelings with uplifting ones. Tarot and journaling can assist you in healing painful moments.

I mention this exercise last because it can bring out strong or intense feelings. Take care. If you find yourself unable to get over the pain, please stop what you are doing and seek out the comfort or help of a loved one, clergy member, doctor, or mental health professional. This exercise may take some time, so I recommend you break it down into manageable chunks.

Pick an event you wish to rewrite. Sit with the memory as it happened. Bring the moment in full color to the forefront of your mind. Recall the scents, the colors, the people. Allow yourself to fully experience it as if it was happening again. (Note: if you begin to feel extreme negative emotions, stop this exercise immediately. It may be too painful for you to work through this right now.) Be present with this experience. Let the feelings wash over you—you are safe, this moment cannot harm you again.

With the event fresh and fully recreated, reach out for your deck. Shuffle the cards, and draw two. The first card tells you why the event was needed in your life. The second card tells you the lesson learned. Look closely at each card as you uncover and unpack the meanings of the cards and the symbols.

When you feel ready, write down the details of the event, and the lesson you learned from it. This may take a while. When you're done, get up and go outside or treat yourself to a cup of coffee. You've done some good work.

Feeling well enough to continue? Good. Take a deep, deep breath and let's move on.

Hold the deck in your hands. Now that you've experienced the full force of the past, how would you rather this period be remembered? Think about how you want to feel. For some, a sense of peacefulness might come to mind. Others may want to turn their rage into happiness. Another good feeling may be forgiveness.

When you have a replacement in mind, turn the deck over and go through the images. You're going to find one or two cards that share the vibe you want. Keep looking until you have the perfect cards. If you're not sure, you can look up card meanings for inspiration.

With your "new feelings" cards, we are going to go back in and explore the event once more. Close your eyes and think about what happened. This time, I want you to change the ending based on the cards you selected. Feel empowered. Allow what happened to loosen up and shift. You are in control now and can replace the negative with a positive.

Rewrite the outcome until you are comfortable with the new feeling. Know you can safely put this moment to rest and let it go so you can move forward with your life. This is not easy to do, so keep in mind that this step of the process can be repeated a few times until you can fully change the way you feel about the event.

Open your eyes. Write down what happened once more. This time, focus on the change you and the cards made. Write about how you feel about the past. Describe the cards you pulled. How did they help you overcome the moment? Was it the overall atmosphere of the card? Perhaps you honed in on a single symbol to use against the memory. Record what drove you to recognize the change.

You now have permission to rewrite any painful memories you may have.

Your Tarot PDA

Recording card meanings and exploring your mind's depths is a fine use of journaling. I want to introduce you to one more type of record keeping. This is the one that feeds my need to keep all the information I know (in a given moment) in one spot. I'm a huge fan of grimoires. They're like the ultimate guides to magic, right? We usually view them as old, musty, hand-bound books costing a lot from obscure bookstores. All the experts have one, don't they?

For our purposes here, yours won't cost an arm and a leg to buy or make. I've been calling books of this type Tarot Personal Data Assistants, or PDAs. Your PDA is like your smartphone in that it keeps important information regarding your tarot practice at the ready when you are out and about. It keeps all your discoveries organized in a way to keep your studies current. Tarot PDAs track *all* the information. Want to track every tidbit of card lore? Done. Want to record all the readings you've ever done? Done. Keep a huge list of all the spreads you found in books, online, or heard from friends? Done. You can also add rituals, games, emergency numbers, and other go-to resources.

Your tarot PDA can take many forms: a physical journal with pages, a three-ring binder, or an app on your electronic devices. Mine has evolved over the years. In 2001, my first tarot PDA was a bound 8.5 by 11-inch lined blank book I got for cheap at the bookstore. I printed out personally meaningful tarot card images and glued them to the cover. Then I labeled each page "The Fool," "The Magician," and so on. After these pages, I added a section for spreads, which spiraled into addied sections for rituals, games, and a small list of go-to websites and books. I completely filled the whole journal with most of what I knew, but unfortunately it became unusable due to its bulkiness!

My next incarnation took form in a disc-bound system. These notebooks use round plastic discs in various sizes bought from office supply stores. Disc-bound journals rock. Unlike a bound book or a spiral notebook, you can pull pages out, move them around, and add more pages in. Like accessories? There's so many to choose from: pockets, tabs, and zip pouches. You can buy pages in many sizes and layout styles. Even the notebooks have different types, and there are specialized punches for printing out your own sheets. Since my first PDA ended up big and unwieldy, my second version went on a diet. I used an index-card-sized notebook. I bought a secondary deck of cards and used a matte white paint to "blank out" the card backs. Once the paint dried, I wrote my personal meanings on them. (An alternative to using paint is finding labels that fit the entire tarot card back. Stick the label onto the card, trim down to size.) I then added tabs for spreads, reading records, and rituals. For many years, this became my grab and go tarot notebook.

These days, you can digitize your thoughts thanks to the advent of smartphone technology. I use Scrivener, my favorite writing app (which I also used to write this book), made folders, and stuffed all the bits of learned info I wanted to keep into pages.

No matter what shape your tarot PDA takes, the key is finding a configuration that allows you to efficiently *use* the tool. Remember that your PDA goes where your tarot decks go; make sure it's a size, shape, and style you like. This tool is your best friend, teacher, and personal assistant—someone you can quickly call upon when you need to know that small snippet of tarot lore you knew you wrote down somewhere.

Using your tarot PDA helps you grow as a reader. Recording all the things you learn is not a static discipline; I've shaped and reshaped my card impressions over the years. Keeping a tarot PDA allows you to parse the data and gives you a long-view perspective of where you were and what you currently see, and perhaps gives insight into where you will go next in your tarot studies. Eventually you may find your stride on what to keep and where to keep it.

For further study and reflection on the topics included in this chapter, look to the following books:

Baldwin, Christina. *Life's Companion: Journal Writing as a Spiritual Quest*. New York: Bantam Books, 1990.

Braden, Nina Lee. *Tarot for Self Discovery*. St. Paul, MN: Llewellyn Publications, 2002.

Jette, Christine. *Tarot Shadow Work*. St. Paul, MN: Llewellyn Publications, 2000.

Kenner, Corrine. *Tarot Journaling: Using the Celtic Cross to Unveil Your Hidden Story*. St. Paul, MN: Llewellyn Publications, 2006.

Chapter 5

Inspiring the Muse
Fun Ways to Play With Your Deck

By the end of this chapter you'll:

- Personalize your tarot decks by resizing or painting them

- Make fabric and crochet cases and cloths for your cards

- Use tarot as an ultimate story generator for plots, characters, and settings

Tarot is an integral part of my life. Whenever I begin learning a new hobby, I am inevitably led to wonder how it could be integrated it into my tarot life. Take crochet, for example. Every time I buy a tarot deck without a tuck box, I go looking for an appropriate case (tuck boxes are great storage containers for decks, and not having a proper container for my cards annoys me). I worry about my new precious getting wet, destroyed, or sticky. So in the past when I couldn't find a suitable container to keep my newly treasured deck in, I turned to something I'd never done before—yarn arts.

Creating clothing to put your cards is just one example of how you can get creative with tarot. Ready to see what else you do with them?

Benefits of Creativity and Tarot

Delving in the creative arts while learning tarot has a few benefits:

Connect to tarot itself. Being creative with tarot allows you to shine. Your personality, individual artistic tastes, and perspective tell you what you like and dislike. Everything interacts when you look at the cards and their shapes and colors and explore the artistic textures. The colors you choose, the items you surround the cards with, and your arrangements all have meaning—they represent your personal expression and show others how you connect to the spiritual world.

Connect to the archetypes. In the process of making tarot-focused art, you'll research each tarot personality. You'll uncover their strengths and how they can benefit you and your life. You'll discover which cards you like and which ones make you uncomfortable. You'll learn to turn negative feelings into powerful aids that can help make you a better person.

Increase your creativity. When you play with the cards and indulge in artistic activities, you develop the hemisphere of your brain that relies on intuition, spatial abilities, and holistic thought. Creativity helps you solve problems, builds your personality, and increases happiness. When you nurture your inner artist, you're not only building connections with the cards, you're also helping your mind grow and your personality shine.

Getting Artsy

Creativity and tarot go hand in hand. From talented artists who paint and design their own decks to writers who create stories based on each card's characters, the images on the cards inspire. Think you're not creative? This chapter will help you see otherwise. It's time to revisit those early playful days of your childhood, and we're going to use all sorts of art supplies to: personalize your deck, make a stand to rest your cards on, and craft pocket shrines.

Personalizing a Tarot Deck

Tarot decks come in many sizes and shapes. There are miniaturized decks requiring a magnifying glass to view the images clearly, and cards so large they require a wall to perform a reading. Personalizing your deck can be as simple as making your deck smaller or enlarging it to fit your hands. In this section, we'll explore the art of resizing your deck through cutting and trimming.

Tarot decks are as sacred as you want them to be. Taking scissors or a trimmer to a prized deck isn't for everyone, but there is a large movement within the community who are willing to get crafty with their decks. Some remove the borders. In order to resize your deck, you'll need the following items:

- A deck to resize. Borders can be culled from any deck. Do use caution when you're cutting rare or expensive decks. If you're not precise in your slices, the card backs can look awkward. Practice on used decks or mock-ups printed out at home. Don't go ruining prized possessions.

- A paper cutter. Buy one with a sharp edge. I prefer Fiskars brand paper cutters, which are carried by many art supply stores.

- A corner rounder. Unless you're fine with sharp corners on your cards, you'll want one of these handy punches. These vary by style and shape. Do some research before purchasing one, as you want to make sure the rounder can cleanly cut through the deck's card stock.

- Ruler. You'll need this for accurate measurement and drawing straight lines.

Practice using your tools before you make the first cut on a card. I'm a perfectionist so I use a ruler and measure the width and length of the cards. (Measure twice and cut once!) Use those spare cards which come with most decks to test your first trims. Mark the borders off with the ruler and then trim using your paper cutter. Does the backside please you? Then move onto cutting the other cards in the deck. You are free to pray or hold your breath as you try this out.

When all the cards are trimmed, use the corner rounder to round each card's edge.

Once all the corners are rounded, take the resized deck for a test drive. Shuffle and do some test readings.

Did you trim the cards to remove the names and numbers? You can re-add them using Sharpie pens or other permanent markers. Further modify your deck by adding glitter, repainting areas with acrylic inks, or use permanent stamp ink on the card edges to give them a weathered look.

Maybe you want your cards bigger. I have a few options for you as well.

Paste a card onto cardboard cut to fit the size you want. You can decorate the new border to fit your style. Make sure you use glue designed to keep the card adhered to the cardboard. When finished, round off the corners, or get the deck laminated.

Buy plastic card holders from online trading card stores. I have never done this, but I do know the sleeves come in many different sizes. You can find ones with graphics printed on their backs.

Wooden Stands

When I work tarot magic, I put my cards on stands where I can
see the images during the meditation or ritual I'm performing.
Books work well, but any pets around can easily scatter the
cards. This wooden card stand keeps cards I'm working with
upright and out of range of the cats.

You can further customize the stand to hold one, three, or
as many cards as you want in a row. A single card stand works
great for meditation, while a twelve-card stand is perfect for
year-long workings.

Here's what I did:

1. Buy wood. I generally get a two by four, which
   can be shortened and resized with a saw. My
   stands are oak because I love the grain and color,
   and I have an affinity for the trees.

2. Measure out the length. You can eyeball this by
   setting down the board and placing the number of
   cards you want the stand to hold. This way you get
   an exact idea for how long the stand can be and
   how much space you want in between the cards.

3. Mark the length and width with a ruler.
   My stands are usually an inch wide.

4. Use a saw to cut the wood; table saws work great
   for this. First cut the length, then the width.

5. This is the tricky part: cut a groove drown the center with a saw. The groove holds the cards in place so you can see them. Make sure your cut is deep enough to keep the card upright but not too deep. You don't want to split the stand in half.

6. Sand the wood. Sanding removes slivers and smooths the wood down so you won't scratch your cards or get slivers in your hands

7. Optional: Stain or paint the wood. Whether you use a colored or clear finish, staining can help protect your wood.

Crafting Pocket Shrines

Make Altoid tin or small box shrines to house tarot energy. These pocket shrines mix your personality with the messages each tarot card offers in a discreet package. One of the smallest decks you can purchase is the Tiny Tarot, whose tiny cards fit perfectly inside an Altoid tin creating fun and portable ways to carry your cards around. Portable shrines are physical representations of what you believe and can be used as sacred study space outside the daily grind no matter where you are.

Design your pocket shrines with a multitude of specific intentions. I have one which goes with me to festivals that's designed to honor the five elements. I made another designed to boost my writing and creative inspiration. That one sits on my desk, ready for me when I write or make art. Want to bring more prosperity into your life? Place money and cards that remind you of prosperity and carry it around as you work.

Pocket shrines are ultimately dual-purpose, both spiritual tool and artistic expression. Since pocket shrines look to the untrained eye like three-dimensional works of art, you can use them to build a relationship with your cards without fear of being ostracized. They give you a safe and covert tool to hide prayers or intentions from prying eyes. Casual observers don't need to know what's in the shrine. When you open it, you get a sacred and personal space to connect to tarot.

Researching and Gathering Materials for Your Shrine

Making shrines is fun and easy. Taking the time to think about the purpose for your shrine takes it from being a piece of art to an integral part of your spiritual practice. In doing so, you'll want to take time to think about the purpose of the shrine. What effect will it have? What cards will you use?

Review the notes in your tarot PDA about the card or cards you want to use. I'll often daydream about what the shrine looks like, what message it holds, and where it'll live in my home.

Turning to the internet can generate more ideas. When I was crafting my magical shrine, I used my knowledge of magic, the books I owned, and various correspondence websites for help in selecting items. I talked to friends about the project for their input and encouragement. I gathered brightly colored papers, images that reminded me of the elements, and other various items together. To this day, when I look at my creation,

I'm amazed at how accurately it represents my connection to the elements and my magic.

Got the right vibe of your shrine? It's time to move onto the second step: gathering ephemera. Ephemera are all those papers, bottles, and "stuff" used to give your shrine purpose and connection. In this stage, anything goes! I've used pictures cut out from magazines or printed from the web, decorative scrap-booking papers for backgrounds, small envelopes, old earrings, beads, tiny art jars, sticks, and so on. Grab items that catch your eye and fit your aesthetic.

At the end, you may find yourself with an overwhelming stockpile of ephemera for the shrine, which is perfectly normal. I go overboard in gathering items to use in my art projects. However, remember that Altoid tins are tiny, about 2" wide by 3.5" long. Obviously this means that not all the items you've gathered are going to get used and/ or fit. At this point you may want to simplify and narrow down your selections, though the exact number of items you want to keep depends on the size of the ephemera you've gathered. But how do you decide what stays and what goes? Turn to tarot and use a simple "in or out" exercise.

Line up each item or put them in piles of similarity. Invoke the spirit of your intent into yourself. Call out to the spirits you want to work with, ask them to be present with you, and to guide you as you build your shrine. Take a few deep breaths to connect with them. Once you feel their presence, shuffle your deck and place a card next to each item or pile. Look at which cards show up. The items with more positive cards next to them will stay. The ones with negative vibes go.

You might need to repeat this whole process a couple of times until you have just enough items (along with a few extra, just in case the design changes) to make a pleasing arrangement inside the shrine.

Making Your First Shrine

These next sections walk you through making your first shrine. I recommend gathering the following items:

- One empty Altoid tin (any size can work, I like the big index card sized ones)

- Ephemera

- Glue stick

- Scissors

- E-6000 or Diamond Glaze brand glues

- Acrylic paint in your favorite colors

- Optional: Polymer oven-bake clay

First, prep the Altoid tin:

1. Wash the box. Decide whether you want to decorate the top of the tin and how to do it. You can leave it as is, paint it with acrylic paints, or use polymer clay to make a cap that fits over the lid.

2. Keeping the tin's appearance "as-is" is a great way to keep your shrine as inconspicuous as possible. Don't feel sad if you settle on this style. It will serve you well, especially if the shrine lives in your office. If you're not altering the outside, move to the next section.

3. Decorate the lid. You can paint the top, or try out a polymer clay cap:

    • Mold a polymer clay cap for your shrine. This clay cap covers the branding and adds dimension. Soften one pack of polymer clay. When it's nice and pliable, cover the lid with a thin layer (don't forget the sides). Keep the hinges free of clay.

    • Optional: Sketch designs, runes, or sigils into the lid with a toothpick or pencil. Dust the top with glitter, or make an impression with a stamp.

    • Place the tin on a cookie sheet and bake it in your oven according to the clay's directions. Depending on the cap's thickness, this can take between four and ten minutes. Let the tin completely cool after removing it from the oven.

4. Decorate the base. I prefer to hide the nutritional information on the bottom, so I use black acrylic

paint and coat the sides and bottom of the shrine in one or two thick layers.

Crafting the Insides

After the tin has cooled and the paint has dried, it's time for the fun part—designing and constructing the inner shrine layout. Which way will your shrine sit—open like a book or will you keep the base tray down. Consider where you will place your shrine to help determine the orientation.

Bring out your ephemera. Look at all the items you've collected to put in the shrine. Chances are that even after the divination exercise, you'll still have more items than may fit into the small space. That's okay; it happens to me when I set out to make a new shrine. I've got lofty ideas and collect so much, but when it comes to arranging and putting it all together, not all those items will work. Breathe deeply. Trust your intuition.

Separate all your items into three piles: background papers, images and flat items, and three-dimensional items (rocks, branches, jars, and so on).

Crafting happens in layers: selecting and adding background paper into both the inside lid and bottom sides of the shrines; adding images and flat items to the background; and finally, adding in the three-dimensional items. Take your time, have fun making the art, and allow yourself to play with each stage as you work on your shrine.

Helpful Tip: Don't glue items into the shrine right away. Test drive designs before pasting down. Bring the tarot into the layout process by laying out some cards to see how they react to the overall design or items. You might be surprised to hear what they have to say!

Decorative background papers: The base of the tin can be a tracing template to size papers to fit inside the tin lids. Layer two or three complementary patterns, and if you need to, glue the paper layers together with a glue stick before permanently attaching them to the inside of the box. If you're layering paper together, wait a few more minutes before attaching the finished piece to the inside.

Use Diamond Glaze or E-6000 to attach the final paper to the backs of both sides of the tin. Press the papers firmly into place, and use your fingertips to clear out any air bubbles. Wait a few minutes before moving on to give the adhesives time to bond the paper to the metal.

Adding images and flat items: Grab all the flat ephemera you have: tarot cards, leaves, flat sticks, coins, etc., and set them onto the background papers. Move each item around and look at the composition. Keep adding or removing items until you're satisfied with the appearance. Layer images on top of one another or on thick pieces of cardboard for a three-dimensional effect.

Use your paint or pens to draw symbols, or sigils, on the papers or images. When you are done, glue all your items down.

This is where you leave enough room to embed those tiny tarot cards. Make and paste a small envelope into the space to create a pocket for the cards you're working with so you can carry them wherever you go.

Adding dimensional items: Let's get dimensional! Place these items inside the tin. Don't just use the bottom of the tin, use the top and sides as well. Arrange all the items you want to include and then glue them all down. I've used all sorts of items in my altars: small statues, bottles filled with dirt and water, old earrings, crystals, and more. I've even made tiny polymer clay offering bowls. Diamond Glaze works great on the lighter items, but for the heavier items you will need to use E-6000.

Hammer or drill a hole in the top of your shrine to dangle objects. In my magical shrine, I took a dreamcatcher earring hoop and threaded it along with some colorful beads through the hole so it could dangle freely in the middle. When I'm away from home, I know my dreams are safe with the spinning mini-catcher at work.

Let your shrine sit overnight when you're done securing all the items in place. If you don't, pieces of your carefully chosen design can fall and peel away.

Making Fabric Tarot Cases

Not all decks come wrapped in nice tuck boxes to keep them secure. Sewing, knitting, or crochet comes in handy when you want a custom bag to store your cards in. I'm not big on the fabric arts but I have made many different bags using basic sewing techniques. Tarot gave me an excuse to learn crochet. In this section, I'll share two designs for you to make cases for your decks. The first, requires minimal sewing and can be done by hand. The second can be easily crocheted.

Sewing a Case

Sewing a slip case is easier than you think. Use the instructions below to sew one by hand or with a machine.

Materials:

- A fat quarter in a print you like. Each bundle gives you enough material for two cases. Fat quarters are small, pre-cut packs of fabric, usually 18" x 22". You can find them at your local craft store and they are an economical way to purchase textiles in fun patterns.

- Heavy cord for the draw string.

- Thread. Make sure the thread is thick enough to withstand the weight of your deck.

- Needle and thread, or a sewing machine.

Making the Bag:

1. Size the fabric. Measure the height, width and depth of the deck. I use a piece of fabric about 10" wide by 9.5" long. This gives a one inch seam allowance for the draw string pocket and some space for sewing the sides together. This pattern fits most standard-sized decks. If the deck you're using is larger or smaller than this, you'll want to adjust your piece of fabric. This pattern wasn't meant to be snug, so if you want to secure your deck, adjust measurements accordingly.

2. Cut the fabric with scissors. Iron your cloth for a nicely pressed look.

3. From here on out, you'll be working with the backside of the fabric. You'll be sewing on this side so the leftover fabric stays hidden inside the case.

4. Fold the fabric in half, lengthwise.

5. Sew one side to make the case using your needle and thread (or the sewing machine). Flip the case over and sew up the other side. This creates the walls of the bag that will hold the deck.

6. Fold the top of the bag down a quarter of an inch. This creates the pocket for the cord to slide through. Sew across the line to attach the pocket to the main body of the bag.

7. Turn the bag right side out again.

8. Thread the cord through the hole and pull the bag closed.

Crochet Case

This pattern fits any standard-sized deck. You can make it wider or taller by adding chains as you see fit. If you don't know how to crochet, there are a lot of instructional videos on the internet.

Materials:

- Desired yarn (worsted weight; I use acrylic and cottons due to allergies)

- Size H hook

- Button (or use polymer clay to bake your own)

Acronyms:
HDC = half-double crochet
CH = single chain

Instructions:

Step one: Chain 14.

Round 1: Two hdc in third chain from hook (2 skipped chains counts as first hdc), hdc in each chain across to end. At the last chain, put 4 hdc in the same hole. Turn the work so you are working on the bottom of the chain.

Put one hdc in each ch to end. Then do a single slip stitch in the top of the first hdc to make the round complete.

Round 2: Chain 2. Put one hdc in back loops of each hdc around. Slip stitch to the top of the first hdc to complete the round.

Round 3 to desired deck size: Repeat round two until you reach the desired length. Do not fasten this off—you'll crochet flap rows next.

Row 1: Chain two. hdc in back loops of each of next 14 stitches. Then chain 2 and turn.

Row 2: Hdc in both loops of each hdc across, then chain 2 and turn.

Repeat row 2 until you have a desired flap length.

Last row: Hdc in loops of 6 hdcs, then chain 2, then hdc in last 6. Fasten off and weave in ends to complete the fabric.

Sew a button on front of bag and close with the flap.

Writing with Tarot

Using tarot to create fictional worlds and as a creativity coach is an absolute joy. In the following sections, we'll go over how this works. By itself, tarot is a book filled with stories and lore in each card. Recall the Fool's Journey from Part One? It exemplifies how using all twenty-two major arcana cards can tell a well-rounded tale. Even the minor arcana contains stories for each suit. Not sure how this works? Go back to part one where we laid out the cards in matrices and see how the story of a suit unfolds one by one.

While tarot contains many stories, in this next part, we'll use all seventy-eight cards to create characters, plots, and settings. We'll also see how the cards can become your writing cheerleading squad and personal coach for inspiration and guidance.

Creating Plot with Tarot

Ease yourself into using tarot and writing by creating a basic story for your future characters. Plot is defined as all the events and action that take your story from start to the end. Tarot imagery is perfect for generating plot ideas because each card you set down can be a singular event. You craft these plots using different spreads. The spreads below are ones I've used time and time again to help shape my novels. You can plot out a whole novel using only the cards, or try using them to create a fast and loose structure to set your characters into.

Plot Generator Templates

These templates range from one card on up and can help you quickly uncover a single scene or thread together your next series. Use them when you are working on new projects or need to revise a current story.

One-Card Quick Story Idea

This spread is pretty much exactly what it says. Take one card at random, or chosen specifically because of the image or the feeling it suggests, and use some aspect of the card to base your whole novel on. All that matters is that this one card sparks an idea for an entire story. If you've already got your plot down, you can use the One-Card Quick Story Idea to create quick events.

Let's say you've drawn a card from the Steampunk Tarot and you see it features a woman in an airship. Can you work an airship encounter into your novel? Perhaps your characters need passage to another world or get hit by a pirate. Perhaps your brain comes up with a totally unrelated idea. What about documenting the tale of a mad scientist who's pouring dangerous liquids into test tubes and selling them as helpful tonics?

Alternatively, this one card becomes a plot point in your story. What's a plot point? This is a scene or event happening inside your book which pushes the story forward. Pull one card and use it to create the next scene for your characters to experience.

Beginning, Middle, End Spread

Three-card spreads are versatile. For our purposes in this chapter, they provide a perfect three-act plot generator: a beginning, a middle, and an end.

The Beginning, Middle, End Layout

The first card acts as the beginning of the book. This can be the opening scene of battle, or the manner in which your character is introduced.

The second card provides the middle of your book. Perhaps this describes the journey your character must take, or gives hints about an item they require. Perhaps, it shows you what needs to happen for the tides to turn in your story.

The last card gives information on how to resolve and wrap up your story. Does it directly relate to how the story ends? Will your story end in happiness or sadness? Look for key symbols you can use.

Short Story Spread

The Short Story spread takes what you learned in the Beginning, Middle, End spread and adds two more cards: conflict and theme. When it comes to stories, conflict is the tension that drives your stories. It's the drama leaving readers turning the pages to find out what happens next! Theme is what truths or meanings your readers should experience and come away with once they've finished reading.

The Short Story Layout

Card One–Beginning: This card represents some aspect of the story's beginning.

Card Two–Middle: This card represents some aspect of the story's middle meat.

Card Three–End: This card represents some aspect of the story's ending.

Card Four–Conflict: This card represents your story's conflict. What motivates your character? Is there another person they have to work with that they don't get along with? This card contains the information for drama in your story.

Card Five–Theme: This card shows you what the theme of your story contains. Will it be about the power of love and how it can conqueror all? Or perhaps you're writing a fairy tale that teaches some sort of modern moral.

The Infinite Story Creation Generator

We will end this section with one final spread, one I like to call the Infinite Story Creation Generator. You can do it alone or with a group of friends. You can use one deck or many. If you're sitting alone, jump down to the next paragraph and begin the experiment. If you are with friends, sit in a circle with your deck(s) in the middle and begin the game.

You are a storyteller who needs to craft stories for your tribe. The muses have left you a tarot deck. You, the wise and imaginative storyteller, take the challenge of using the cards to make your tribe happy.

Before playing, figure out how many rounds to play. Everyone gets to speak in a single round. Determine the number randomly using a number from a card or rolling dice.

Each player picks five cards from a fully shuffled deck. Set a timer for five minutes. This is the length of time each player has to fully craft a story. When the timer is up, the first story teller goes.

Look at your hand. Weave as many cards together in a coherent storyline as you can. You are allowed to rearrange the cards. Think about how the scene in the first card might get to the scene in the next card and so on. Doing this exercise helps you strengthen your ability to weave scenes and later write entertaining and educating stories.

You can opt to get help from others. You gain one point for accepting outside suggestions as well as one point per card not used in the story.

Once the storyteller finishes, add up the score. Then the next player gets to tell their story.

After the pre-determined rounds have been played, the game is done. The person with the lowest points wins and gets crowned Grand Poobah.

Creating Characters with Tarot

Characters are your story's actors, and readers follow along their journey. Stories contain three types of characters: protagonists, antagonists, and minor characters. A protagonist is the focal point of the story, the hero of the book, and typically your main character. The antagonist is the opposition to your main character: an adversary, the one who interferes with your story's world. Together, the two provide the drama and tension your book needs to keep the reader turning pages. Finally, minor characters provide background and filler to your story. These characters run into your protagonists, help them on occasion, and interact in small but profound ways to move your protagonists along in their personal development.

Tarot is a perfect tool for crafting fun, colorful, and interesting characters no matter what category they fall into. When creating characters with the cards, let any aspect of the card inspire you. I've used colors off the cards to designate a character's favorite color, or the way characters dress in multiple decks to figure out my characters' attire. I've even used the card numbers to designate character ages. When it comes to creating characters, you don't need to know what the cards mean—they are starting points for your imagination.

Character Creation Templates

These character spreads are templates that vary using one up to many cards. They can quickly uncover minute details of your character, such as hair or eye color, all the way to their temperament when dealing with the stresses and hurdles you toss at them. Consider them quick character profiles for the people in your worlds.

One-Card Trait Spread

The One-Card Trait Spread is designed to give you an overall character idea. From hair color and length to eye color to height and age, it can help rough out your characters. Particularly inspiring tarot figures can influence a character in your story. Use a single card to define a unique visual signature: clothing style, posture, walk, or mannerism. Use a card's meaning to describe a back-story idea, strength, flaw, or motivator for your character.

For example, let's say I draw the Four of Pentacles. On a standard Rider-Waite-Smith deck, this card features an image of a man sitting in a chair. He has one coin resting on top of his head and two trapped under his feet. He grasps a fourth coin in his hands. It appears as if he's clutching it quite closely. Given this information, I can immediately discern a few ideas about a character to create: he's male, likes to hang onto money closely, perhaps likes to dress in fine garments, is in his forties (for this I took the number four and decided to add on a few decades), and has a scarcity mentality. He's afraid all his items will be taken from him. Any and all of these ideas could be used to help me create an interesting character for a story.

Simple Four-Card Character Spread

In this four-card spread, we draw cards to represent various aspects of the character.

The Four Card Character Layout

Card One–Visual Trait. Something on this card becomes a part of your character. Perhaps the colors define their eye hue. Maybe it defines your character's gender. Look back to the One-Card Trait spread for a long list of ways you can view this card to draw out a character's appearance.

Card Two–Main Strength. This card addresses your character's main strength. What makes this character likable? Are they smart, good with puzzles? Is their constitution strong? Just like reality, your characters have a list of qualities they consider their strengths. This card can help you pick one for them.

Card Three–Main Flaw. What flaw does your character have? Like it or not, no one is perfect. Is your character stingy or do they hoard money? Do they have a hard time letting go of physical possession? Perhaps their flaw is more psychological in that they are scared of the world and have a hard time standing up for themselves and what is right. Good stories and good characters use strengths and flaws that play off one another, keeping the audience wondering what happens next.

Card Four–Motivation. The motivator card gives you input on your character's primary motivations. What drives your character? Is it money, fame, or relationship desire? This is a really fun one to come up with because you have to honor this agreement as you write the character's tale. You cannot swap motivations or force this character to do something they would refuse to do. Real people don't work that way, so why should your characters?

Creating Settings with Tarot

A setting is the location, timeline, or social institution your story takes place in. Setting colors the language your characters use, the clothing they wear, and the technology, or social structures.

Setting Creation Templates

In these spreads, you'll generate whole worlds or aspects of places for your characters. Quickly uncover locations, build cities or continents, and select time periods to set your story in. Create worlds featuring fantastic biospheres and intricate cultures. Use these templates when you want some help to spice up your story settings.

One-Card Location Creator

Draw a single card to generate a quick location. Use elements on this card to visualize a place. Draw your ideas from the landscapes painted on the card. Does the card show a building or a wide open pasture? How could this setting help or hinder your characters and their quest?

Four-Card Location Creation Spread

As a final spread to give you to understand how the cards can help you create fast, fun and interesting locations for your stories to take place within, I want to introduce the Four-Card Location Creation spread. Like the Character Profile spread, this spread is designed to give you a well-rounded location for your story. It asks that you draw four cards that represent aspects of a single location to make realistic places.

The Four-Card Location Layout

Card One: Geographical Location. Where is this place located? Sometimes the cards depict city settings or wide open desert vistas. No matter what deck you use, figure out where in the world/universe it resides.

Card Two: Year/Time Period. What epoch or time period is your story set in? Will your characters fit in a medieval world or a Victorian-type era? Does your world have a contemporary vibe? Select a card and see what sorts of information about the year or era it can show.

Card Three: Atmosphere. What general vibe does this location have? Coffee houses may appear light and airy, with many people sitting at tables typing away. Or perhaps you receive a dark, gloomy, and spooky forest vibe containing many unknown sounds and sights. Draw a card to try figuring out what the card's atmosphere is and how it can be used to give your location its vibe.

Card Four: Season/Weather. This card represents the season or weather conditions taking place at the location while your characters are there. Are your characters prepared for eternal winter conditions? This card is great for books that involve lots of quests or trips. Draw a card for each location they visit throughout their travels.

With these spreads, you have all you need to start writing your story. They work for all genres and prime the pump for knocking out first drafts quickly. Next up we'll look at how tarot can become a writing coach and cheerleader. After all, writing doesn't have to be a solitary act, even though many view it as such.

Your Tarot Coach

Writers spend thousands on writing books, editors, book designers, and coffee. With tarot, we can spend less (maybe; I seem to have a book addiction) and get immediate, tangible answers on our projects. It's amazing what a small deck of cards can do. In this section we'll look at spreads and ways that tarot can encourage you, help you brainstorm new ideas, and help you decide on your next project.

Tarot has seventy-eight unique perspectives—that's a lot of individual support, advice, and ideas. So, why wouldn't you want to put your deck to use as your own support team?! No matter which card comes up, you'll get good ideas to keep you motivated, focused, and on target for hitting the goals you want.

If your mind hasn't given you a ton of ways to use your deck as a coach, here are a few spreads and ideas to get you started.

One-Card Questions

Some days, I'm not focused. I sit staring at a blank page and the words don't come. Editing whole chapters seems daunting. Sometimes when I've finished a project, I wander around aimlessly, wondering what to do next. On these days I take out my deck and ask simple questions (and if the cards are lucky, we do this over hot chocolate). I ask my cards the following:

- How am I doing?

- What should I work on next?

- What are my strengths as a writer?

- What writing weaknesses (or work weaknesses) need to be worked on? (This question usually has follow-ups to pinpoint specifics.)

Creative Advice Spread

This spread takes a snapshot of your creative life. While this spread appears in the writing section of this chapter, you can use it for visual or audio creative arts as well. The four positions help determine: your blocks, new ideas, where the passion lies, and what your next step is. When I go through long periods of not creating content, this spread reminds me why I do what I do and how I can be a better writer.

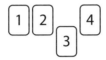

The Creative Advice Layout

Card One: Brainstorm. What project sounds interesting to me?

Card Two: Expression. What idea do I want to express?

Card Three: Blocks. What's blocking my creativity? Use this card to identify a block keeping you from starting, completing, or moving on to the next project.

Card Four: Stepping Stone. What's your next step? This is a concrete action step; commit to doing this action.

Your Own Personal Cheerleader

Writing is hard work. You develop your writing chops by placing one word in front of the other, and you keep going until you have exhausted all the possibilities of how to say what you want to say. Non-writers have a distorted view of writing as being easy; they imagine writers dump glorious prose onto the page perfectly the first time. As one who has written stories, poems, essays, technical documentation, and little white books her entire life, I call bull-honkey! Writers struggle with "work" just like anyone else. Some days it's hard to even craft an email.

When you have a case of the doldrums, you can also turn to your deck to help with a pick-me-up. Shuffle the cards. When you are ready, draw a card to see what pep talk the cards can give you. The advice can come in the form of the card's image or a keyword written on the card, or it may not even be from the card at all. Instead, perhaps your cat appears and places its paw on you to tell you it's time to take a break.

Our connections to the cards can instantly cheer us up. One of my favorite cards from the Shadowscapes deck is the Queen of Wands. Every time I see her, she reminds me that writing matters and is my calling. I need to take a deep breath, put my fingers to the keyboard, and keep the words flowing.

Revision and Editing Advice

Writing a first draft is easy compared to revising. You have to take time to re-examine your work, dive back into the world you created, and figure out what is missing. You scrutinize your characters from all the angles and remove the fluff. Cutting your darlings and favorite passages is hard, and watching the effort you put into the draft get cut and slashed can be heart-wrenching.

Other times, re-reading poorly written passages makes you cringe and want to throw in the towel. If you're wondering where you begin making it all better, it's time to bring out your deck and draw some cards.

A great place to start is to ask "What should I focus on first in revising this draft?" See what advice your coach gives you. Will it tell you to tighten up the characters or fix scene pacing? Maybe it tells you to put the draft away for a while so you can return to it with fresh perspectives. This gives you a path, a focus, a lifeline to grab onto when you feel like the whole thing is just too large and you do not know where to begin.

Submissions and Approaches to Getting the Work Published

You've spent years editing your novel. You've read books on revision and spent countless hours re-imagining your work so even your biggest skeptic loves it. At this point, you're probably thinking it's time to release it into the world. If you are at this step, welcome to the world of publication. As with the other areas of writing, tarot can help you figure out the best route for you to publish your work, and who will give you the best deal while honoring your integrity.

We're fortunate to live in an age where we can become our own publishing company—technology has come a long way. Affordable software and the internet give us outlets to push our works into the hands of eager readers. All you need is an idea, time to write those thoughts down, the knowledge and the ability to convert the book to a digital format, and a website to market, promote, and handle sales. However, not everyone has the drive, desire, and moxie to handle all aspects of their work, which is why traditional publishing is still around.

If this is where you are, perhaps the first question to ask your tarot coach is whether or not traditional publishing is the way to go. You could do a forecasting spread to show you what would happen if you self-published the book, and what would happen if you went with a more traditional path.

For example:

Kendra's on the fence. She doesn't know whether or not she wants to publish her book traditionally or on her own. Her material is good and she's spent a lot of hours editing. To find an answer, she takes out her deck and does a forecasting spread.

The first four cards she lays down represent what could happen if she self-publishes. The first card details the effects of paying for layout and editing. Then she looks at the market for where she'll sell her books. The third card gives her an idea of the market and what her marketing efforts will give her. The final card gives her a baseline measure of how successful her self-publishing efforts will be.

She lays down four more cards. These represent the conditions for submitting with a traditional publisher. The first card gives insight on which firm to select. The second gives her insight into how the company will treat her work. The third gives insight into the marketing and distribution plans. The last card shows her how successful her book will be in the marketplace.

With these points of data, Kendra has a better idea of which route gives her a better option. Sometimes this may be the self-publishing route, and other times it may be going with someone traditional.

Another way the tarot can help you navigate the publication process is in selecting which places to which you submit your query letter. Query letters are letters of intent to publishers you think you'd like to work with. For shorter works this may be submitting your poems or short stories to magazines. For longer works this may include a chapter-by-chapter synopsis, along with a captivating letter.

Before you get your cards involved, research the companies you want to work with. List the company names and any employee contacts. Find out how they treat their authors and what services they provide. Do they help out with marketing? Do they give you advanced reader copies (ARCs) for promotion?

Got a list? Pull a card or two for each company. Write the names of the cards down next to the name of the company. Use the insight to give you an idea on whether or not the firm is a good fit for you. Once you've drawn cards for every publisher on your list, look at the similarities and contrasts to see which place may give you the best deal.

For further study and reflection on the topics included in this chapter, look for the following books:

Couturier, Andy. *Writing Open the Mind.* Berkeley, CA: Ulysses Press, 2005.

Crisspin, Jessa. *The Creative Tarot.* New York: Touchstone, 2016.

Elford, Jaymi. "Spirits on the Go." in *Engaging the Spirit World.* Stafford, UK: Immanion Press, 2013.

Kenner, Corrine. *Tarot for Writers.* Woodbury, MN: Llewellyn Publications, 2009.

McElroy, Mark. *What's in the Cards for You?.* St. Paul, MN: Llewellyn Publications, 2005.

Chapter 6

Getting Spiritual
Seeking Inner and Higher Truths

By the end of this chapter you'll:

- Understand meditation basics

- Use tarot imagery for meditation

- Explore the cards with a guided meditation

- Use the cards to communicate with the divine and/or other entities

In these next three chapters, we turn our attention from tarot as an everyday companion and move toward building a spiritual path. Performing readings and receiving questions about your life is fun, but so is using the cards to ask the deeper questions. Questions like "Why am I here" or "What can my higher self do to help me through this transition?" bring depth to your tarot studies.

As with the other areas in this book, we build up your practice step-by-step. We start our journey by going within. I'll give you some basic meditation techniques to try out. We then add your cards to the mix, and see what is inside you. We'll then expand this more by introducing the idea of becoming the archetypes using a blend of cosplay and math. I'll also give you ideas of how to use the cards and a pendulum to chat with various spiritual guides and entities.

Basic Meditation Techniques

Meditation can feel like an elusive guide to enlightenment to some. Everyone says it's good for you, and it is. But we still shy away from it. I'll admit, I'm no expert. In fact, you can say I'm a fair-weather meditator—I don't do it daily or have a regular, set schedule. Disclaimers aside, I have an uncomplicated and flexible process. We'll go over them in the exercises.

Before I settle down to meditate, I pick a time and place with low ambient noise. The cell phone, the TV, and the internet get turned off so I can relax in the moment. I alternate between lying down and sitting up for my meditation sessions; the position isn't terribly important. The point is to find a comfortable and relaxing body posture that doesn't induce sleep or pain.

If there's one reason to use an electronic device during meditation, it's as a timer. There are some pretty nifty meditation apps out there, but what you use must be minimal and distraction free. You don't want to waste your time playing with the app instead of keeping your eyes closed. Timed meditations are good when you have a busy schedule and want to clear your head of noise. Even a quick five-minute meditation helps you focus.

On the other hand, simply sitting down, closing your eyes, and letting the mind meander for unspecified periods of time can be beneficial as well. Meditations of this sort detox your mind of speed. It's a reset button on your day, giving you time to slow down and quiet the doubts and noise going on around you.

EXERCISE: KNOW YOUR BODY

Knowing your body is key to establishing a meditation practice. If meditation is a process of stilling one's mind, having a relaxed body helps promote this awareness.

In this exercise, you'll position your body in various postures to see how your body responds to them. Specifically, we're looking for any sore or painful spots, as these "red alert" signals make it harder for the mind to let go and release awareness. They draw your attention from the abstract moment. The more you know about your body, the more you understand how to avoid placing it in positions that trigger pain and discomfort.

People relax differently. If you find sitting lotus position doesn't work for you, move on to another arrangement. When you find the right orientation, your brain lets go. Relaxing gives your brain a break from worrying about life's details. It opens up instead to new ideas, possibilities, and creations.

Don't force yourself into any of the below poses—this isn't gym class. If your body hurts, stop and move into the next position. Our goal here is promoting awareness. Try each situation for no longer than five minutes. Go through each rotation once a day for a whole week.

As you try each one out, pay attention to your body. Do your nerves go nuts? Are there any pain spots? Keep these in mind. If it hurts to bend or twist, or if you can't stand up from it, cross it off the list.

- Lie down in bed or on the floor.

- Sit down in a chair. Try out multiple chairs: your desk chair, a wooden chair, a barstool. See if the type of chair you sit in promotes or detracts from being relaxed.

- Sit lotus style on the floor.

- Go outside and walk around. Sometimes sitting around isn't relaxing at all. Sometimes moving helps achieve a more relaxed state.

Exercise: Mental Meanderings

Once you learn to trust your body and recognize the effects of the various positions, the next step is to let your mind still. We'll explore two different ways to achieve this in this exercise. I want you try out these techniques like you did in the last exercise. See which one works better for you. Each one affects your mind differently.

Try the first technique daily for two weeks. Then do the same for the second technique. Can you do either one for five minutes? Record your thoughts and experiences in your journal. Which one helps to promote relaxation and clarity?

1. *Focus on your breath.* Focusing on the breath is the easiest way to slip into a meditative state. Draw attention down to the air coming in and going out of your nose, mouth, and lungs. Count to four as the air comes into your nose. Then focus on the air as it exhales out the mouth. You'll be doing another four count here too. Do this slowly and steadily and don't hold your breath. You want the airflow to be steady. Too fast makes you hyperventilate; too slow and you get light-headed. When thoughts pop into your head, try not to pay attention to them. Keep your focus on your breathing. If you find that you are losing your ability to just focus on your breath, gently bring your intention back to your breath and continue on.

2. *Imaginative wanderings.* I call this the "window shopping" technique. In this situation, you allow all the thoughts to flow into your head. You can take a second to view what is going on but cannot grab onto it and dive deeper. The point is practicing detachment. Whatever pops into your mind, note its appearance and hop to the next memory. This technique sounds easy, but our minds are susceptible to reliving and holding onto memories—it's harder than you think. If negative thoughts and memories appear, stop the session immediately. Think about happier moments and try this technique another day.

It's very easy for beginners to lose focus on the breath and get lost in the deluge of thoughts and images the mind conjurers up. I know this well; it happens to me constantly. When it happens, it's best to gently bring focus back to the breath: in through the mouth and out through the nose. Don't beat yourself up for losing focus. Everyone loses focus at some point. Even Buddhist monks in the monasteries high in the clouds of the Himalayans lose their focus.

Tips and Tricks

Put the last two exercises together and you have the recipe for a basic meditation practice. The following are some tips and tricks I've used during my own explorations.

Be easy on yourself. Learning a new skill takes time. (This sounds familiar, right?) While meditating, you'll find your body rebelling against the stillness (mine does constantly). Little sounds become huge. Distractions exist all around you. They want to take you away from your session. This is okay, it's expected. Gently guide your mind back by focusing on your breathing, or turn your attention to something else.

Be consistent. Pick the same time every day. Meditating is an exercise, so you need to build muscle memory as with any exercise. One of the best ways to do this is to train your body to go into a relaxed state at the same time each day.

Give yourself permission to move while meditating. Most meditation books talk about sitting or standing still. While many great meditation formats require your body to be unmoving, sitting still doesn't work well for everyone. I have a restless body and a constantly itchy nose. When I sit down, I shuffle around, stretch my arms, scratch my nose, and sniffle. This is absolutely okay. Trying to hold back all this just makes your body more rebellious. And as we've seen, it's harder to meditate when those alarms are going off and demanding that you deal with that irritation. I've learned I meditate best when I am able to move, even if it's just to rub my finger against a stone or scratch my nose. I also meditate when I exercise at the gym.

Explore other meditation techniques. There are a lot of good books out there that teach a wide variety of techniques. There are group meditations to try or guided meditations you can download. I encourage you to explore those books and see what styles you find best. I include a few at the end of this chapter, so definitely check them out.

Meditating with Tarot

As I see it, there are many ways to meditate with tarot. In this section, we'll test out four different types of meditation techniques involving the cards:

- Card shuffling. Still your mind and be present while shuffling the cards.

- Meaning focus. Learn how to connect to the heart of the card.

- Image exploration. Allow your mind to push beyond the edge of a card.

- Group meditation. Use a script and learn insight from others while meditating.

EXERCISE: SHUFFLING MEDITATION

Shuffling cards is an important part of the reading process. Shuffling randomizes the cards. It helps us focus our energy and intent into the reading process, and it gives us a moment to allow the energies of the universe to open up. Shuffling is also a great introduction technique to meditating with tarot. When I was younger, I'd sit for hours in my room shuffling a deck of cards. This practice of picking the cards up, cutting the deck in half, and letting them fall over each other, was how I taught myself to riffle shuffle.

With this technique, you can forget what you know about tarot— the symbols, their interpretation, spreads. Just focus on holding the cards and moving them back and forth. Riffle shuffling works best for this exercise but you can experiment with other styles of shuffling.

This kind of meditation is quite easy to do. All you need is a deck (any deck will do, even oracle or playing cards). Split the deck into two piles and put one in each hand. Then tilt the piles so you start dropping cards from onto each other. Repeat the shuffle movement until you lose yourself in it. Breathe and keep doing this until you lose yourself.

Exercise: Meaning Meditation

In this technique you'll place your focus on the image and keyword meaning of the card. Set a timer for your preferred session length. Now, draw a card from your deck. Look at the image. How well can you reconstruct the image in your mind? Stare at the picture until you can recreate the whole scene accurately.

Relax and breathe. Close your eyes and recreate the card's imagery in your mind. With the image in mind, allow a meaning or a message come through. Take some time to contemplate this meaning fully.

When your timer goes off or when you feel you have thoroughly explored the card, come back to the present time and give yourself some space for reintegration. If you feel compelled, write down your experience in your journal.

Sample Session

I hold my basic deck in hand and begin shuffling. I pull the Empress. The card's image shows a blonde woman lavishly sitting on a seat full of pillows. Her long white dress is printed with pomegranates. She holds a scepter in her right hand and a shield rests at her feet with the symbol of Venus, a universal symbol of woman. Her seat rests in between a wheat field and a forest that has a waterfall flowing down it. I look at this card and try to memorize as much as possible: the woman, the trees in the background, as many details as I can.

Once I have the complex image in my mind, I start my basic practice. I close my eyes and recreate the image fully. Then I lock the image in place with my mind and attempt to connect to the card. The meanings begin to bubble up: abundance, creativity, being pregnant with ideas, flow.

My key passage for the Empress is creative abundance. Everything on this card is plentiful. As I think about how giving this card is, I focus on how this works in my life. I'm an idea generator. My friends and I exchange ideas for stories, spreads, and projects on a daily basis. During my writing sessions, I use the Empress for creative problem solving.

I hold the picture and the meaning in my mind for as long as my meditation session goes for. When I am done, I stretch my body out and then return back to the present. I give thanks to the powers that allow me to tap into the unlimited source of all that is creative and go back to my daily business. Later, I write about this experience in my journal.

EXERCISE: EXPERIENCING THE CARD

Experiencing the Card is another tarot meditation approach. In this technique, you'll break the borders of the card (quite literally) to envision the larger world. Instead of focusing on the meaning, you'll step into the world and experience it firsthand. Use all your senses with this exercise to become fully present with the card's world.

I've included a script to help guide you into the card. Make a recording of yourself or have someone read the script if it helps you get into the mood.

This is one of my favorite ways to meditate with the cards. I'll pick up my deck and hop into a card to explore for a bit. It gets me out of my current mood and also allows my mind to wander. Stepping into the cards and imagining what the world is like inside is a lot of fun.

When you experience this technique, pick a card from your deck and memorize the image again. When you have that image inside your head, use the basic meditation techniques to begin a meditation session. When you close your eyes and become relaxed, you'll picture the card in your mind and then enter the card to begin exploring it. When you are finished, you might want to write your experiences down.

BEGIN SCRIPT

Take your time. Relax. Focus on all the details in the card. Look for the big symbols first. Memorize them. Start sketching them out in your mind. Now turn to the smaller details. Continue drawing them in your mind. Breathe and relax. Close your eyes. Bring the whole card back into the forefront of your mind. Picture it in your mind. Feel the card growing larger. Bigger. It is a doorway—one you can step into. Breathe and step into the card.

Look around. What do you see? Take a deep breath. What scents are present? Reach out and touch the trees, the items around you. How do they feel? Do you see someone nearby? Walk over to the character. Do they interact with you or ignore you? Breathe. Move around this world. What do you see around the corners of where the borders would appear?

When you are ready, return back through the doorway of the card and back into your body.

END SCRIPT

Sample Session

For example, I used the Three of Cups from the Rider-Waite-Smith deck. I prepared myself by grounding myself to the Earth and opening a connection to my higher consciousness. Once I felt ready, I placed the Universal Waite deck in my hands and began shuffling. I stopped when it felt correct to stop and then I drew a card from the deck, which happened to be the Three of Cups.

I memorized the card so I had a good picture of it in my head. I then put the card into the screen of my mind and when I was ready, I made it bigger so I could walk into the card.

I stepped through the door and saw three witches dancing in a circle with their goblets raised high in the air. Behind the witches appeared a small garden where fall vegetables were growing, many of them ripe for picking. Turning my head to the left, I saw a cauldron resting over red and orange stones and coals, wispy white and grey steam rising from the middle of the of the pot. Turning my head to the right, I saw a wooden bench with a basket sitting on top. Three place settings were also there. I thought a dinner party would commence at any moment.

I heard laughter, hushed speaking, and chanting. I heard the crackling of a fire snapping at the side, low and hot. I heard the hissing of wood as it was consumed by the fire's heat. I heard my belly growl as it was hungry and wanted to have either the pumpkins on the vine or a sip from the cauldron. I heard the sounds of the goblets as they clinked and clanged against one another as the women toasted.

I smelled the sweet scent of dew in the air. I also smelled herbs and meat coming from the cauldron, as if a meal were cooking inside. I smelled the scent of overturned earth and plants that had been removed from their home on the vine. I smelled the light scent of cider sloshing around the cups the three women were carrying.

I tasted the dry air that had been seasoned by ash and wood scent. I tasted the flavors of herbs and meat that were stewing. I tasted the mead the ladies had filled their chalices with.

I felt the softness of the ground beneath my feet and the bristles of each blade of grass. I felt the heat from the burning fire. I felt the roughness of the wood of the table off to the side. I felt the hardness of the vines on which the vegetables ripen on and the softness of the women's hair and dresses as they spun around in circles.

Exercise: Guided meditations around the archetypes (aka group meditations)

A guided meditation is done using a script which is either read out loud to participants or recorded for personal use. Guided meditations take you on a journey. They ask you explore various realms or aspects of yourself, and sometimes include tasks for you to do. Guided meditations have built-in pauses, giving you time and space to follow along with the journey.

The last exercise gave you a small taste of the power behind guided meditations. This exercise expands upon the technique. You can perform the exercise alone, with the help of a recording device, or you can perform it in a group setting.

Meditation scripts exist all over the internet. Some improve focus, others help you sleep. Writing scripts with the cards is a fun and rewarding process. You can focus a guided meditation around one card, several cards, or even base a whole meditation around the entire deck structure. Let the cards and your creativity guide you into what feels right.

The following script is a generic guided meditation I've written. It allows you to meet an archetype, talk to them and see what wisdom they have for you, and receive a gift you can integrate back into yourself to help you.

A Sample Guided Meditation Script

Relax and breathe. Let all the tension of the week leave your body. Inhale deeply. As you exhale, slow your breath down. Feel yourself inside your body. All is safe and secure.

When you are ready, step out of your body. Allow your spirit to float into the sky. Higher and higher you go. Look down, see the world beneath your feet.

Look around. Find a nearby forest. When you've spotted one, descend down into it.

Feel your feet touch the earth. Take a step forward and wander around. Smell the trees and the earth. Press your feet into the soft ground. Look at the trees and underbrush. Look into the sky, notice the time of day. Feel the weather touch your skin. Touch the trees. Feel the roughness of their bark, the smoothness of the leaves. Listen to the sounds of the forest surrounding you. Taste the air. You are perfectly safe in this area.

You see a path. Step onto the path and walk. The path takes you up the side of a mountain. At the top is a cave. Torches line the sides of the entrance. Step off the path and move towards the cave.

Peek inside. More torches line the sides of the walls. The flames flicker across the cave walls. There are paintings on the walls. Move deeper in the cave and read the walls. Try and remember the story.

The passage opens up and the ceiling raises up. The torches dim as you move into the room. In the center of the cavern, a new light grows stronger and brighter. It turns into a warm, inviting fire. Move toward the fire.

A cloaked person sits on the opposite side of the fire. Move closer to the person. Acknowledge and greet them. They gesture for you to sit. You sit down next to them.

Slowly, your companion moves closer to the light and pulls the hood down. You realize, you are in the presence of one of the tarot archetypes. Stare at the archetype. Which one is it?

The archetype greets you and invites you to tell your story. Tell them your story. Watch as they listen attentively.

When you are done, the archetype looks up and tells you their story. They tell you their name. They talk about why they are here and what help they can offer you.

Listen to the archetype. Take their message into your heart.

When the archetype is finished, ask them any questions about what they have just told you. How can they help you in your life?

Thank the archetype for coming to you and being a wise presence in your life. Stand up and get ready to leave.

Feel the archetype reach out to you once more. In their hand appears a token. This is a gift, a symbol of your time together.

Look down at the token and take it. Remember what it is. How can you use this item? How is this gift something you need?

As soon as you memorized the item, it disappears into your body and becomes a part of you.

Thank the archetype once again.

Find your way out of the cave. Torches light back up as you go outside. Step on the path once more and head back down into the woods. Rise up, and push your body back into the sky. Note where you are and locate your body. It calls you home.

Step back into your body. Give your spirit time to settle back into it. Stretch and shake your body.

Take a few minutes to re-orient yourself. When you are ready, open your eyes.

Embodying the Archetypes

Bringing the archetypes and lessons of tarot into your mind is but the first step of bonding with them spiritually. Once you integrate their teachings, you can then manifest them into your own world by embodying them. Embodying the Archetypes combines elements of guided meditation and cosplay to bring the major arcana into your life.

There are four phases to this process. Step one is to calculate your soul or life path cards. Mary K. Greer has written about this extensively (look at the resources in the back of this chapter). It's a wonderful way to make personalized connections with the archetypes. Step two is a research phase where you learn about your chosen archetype. Once you know about your archetype, you can record the guided meditation script or have a group facilitator lead you through a meditation to bring forth the archetype and integrate it with your personality, for a little bit. Then you can use the power of that personality to interact with the world. Use the power of the Emperor to help you in a job interview. Bring Death forward in processing grief. At the end of this process, you'll take some time to journal about the experience.

When I run my students through this work, not only do I have them become the archetypes of the cards, and allow them to move around, talk, and dress as their archetypes desire, I also have them interact with one another as if they were on a talk show. Once the "show" is finished, I lead the archetypes back out of their hosts and allow the students to return to normal once more. The group then spends time journaling about their experience or discussing it among themselves.

Calculate Soul and Life Path Cards

Soul cards represent the energies surrounding a person as they move through life. These are guiding archetypes and have big influences on how you interact with the world. Who you are and how you navigate life is influenced by your cards. My personal soul cards speak to who I am and what I've chosen to do in life. Use the day, month, and year you were born to calculate which major arcana cards are your soul cards.

Life path cards change year to year. These cards represent the energies that surround you during the current year. They are like soul cards but their energies are transitionary, changing each year on your birthday. I've had fun calculating the energies for each year as I get older (and hopefully wiser). To figure out what life path archetype you have, use the current year along with the month and day you were born.

Before you follow this process, decide whether or not you want to calculate your soul cards or life path card. You'll need a calculator, and the twenty-two major arcana cards. Even though the Fool has a number of zero, we use the number 22 as his own card—we don't want to leave the fellow out!

Write down your birth day, month, and year on a piece of paper. Let's say that your birthday is April 25, 1998 and you have decided to do a year card reading for 2010. You would write this down as:

Day: 25

Month: 04

Current year: 2010

Then you add it up. 25 + 04 + 2010 = 2039

The total, 2039, is then reduced down because we're looking for numbers under 22. In this case, 2039 breaks down into a single digit. If two numbers fall between this range, then you have two life path cards for that year.

2 + 3 + 9 = 14

The value of 14 falls in our range, but it can also be reduced:

1 + 4 = 5

Next we reduce 1998, like so:

1 + 9 + 9 + 8 = 27

Since 27 doesn't fit within our range, we reduce it down further:

2 + 7 = 9

The number 9 becomes our life path card. We then flip through our major arcana pile and pull card nine, the Hermit from our deck. Once you have selected your card, you can move onto the Research Phase to continue on with this exercise.

When you calculate your soul path cards, you use the year of your birth to discover your soul path cards.

Multiple Card Example

Not everyone gets a single soul card or life path card; it's possible to have multiple. In this case, we honor and acknowledge all those cards. When going through Embodying the Archetypes process, we focus on one card.

Say your birthday is August 10, 1974.

You would add this up as

Birth date: 10

Birth month: 08

Birth year: 1974

In addition to the earlier example where the year was broken down by individual numerals, you can also add the whole thing together:

10 + 8 + 1974 = 1992

Then we reduce 1992 down like so: *1 + 9 + 9 +2 = 21*

The number 21 falls within our target range, so we know that the first card is 21, or in this case, the World. We don't have to stop there, as 21 can be further reduced to *3: 2 + 1 = 3.* In this case, card 3, the Empress becomes our second card.

Take both of these cards from the tarot deck and look at them to figure out which one you would like to use during the Embodying the Archetypes process. Pick one and then move into the Research phase of the process. Or you can research information about both cards before deciding. Note that by the end of the Research Phase you will have to pick one of the archetypes to work with.

Research Phase

In this phase, you'll hit the books and use research to select personality traits for your archetype personas. The Research Phase works great when you have a lot of tarot books. If you are doing this as a group, place all the books in the center and let everyone pull from the pile. Access the internet for additional information, if you want. I find the internet can be distracting, so don't get too sidetracked.

I like to ask the cards these three questions:

- How do you (archetype) fit into my personal life?

- What challenges and strengths do you have for me?

- How do you manifest as an example in my life?

Don't spend too much time on research. Keep the sessions short, no more than thirty minutes. You don't want the magpies and distractions to get in the way of your focus. If you're doing this in a group, reserve some time to let everyone swap stories.

When everyone is ready, next is the Meditation Phase.

Meditation Phase

In this third phase of Embodying the Archetypes, you'll use a recorded meditation script or have someone take you through. This script helps you fuse your personality with your selected archetype. With the archetype installed, you can use their power to help you in your daily life. If you are doing this in a group, you can ask the archetypes questions and see how they'd interact with one another in a talk show format.

Use the guided meditation in the next section to get connected to an archetype. The full meditation takes about twenty minutes but you can adjust the pace based on your needs and desires.

The questions inside the meditation are placeholders. Depending on which archetypes are with you, you could hold informal interviews with them and watch as they play off of one another. While it has not happened in any of my classes, if you have the more active or violent archetypes (like the Devil and the Tower), control the situation before it gets out of hand. Be prepared to calm things down and separate personalities if discussions get heated or carried away.

When you are finished, return to the script and allow the archetype to leave your mind.

Embodying the Cards Guided Meditation Script

Use this script to safely install various tarot archetypes into your personality. Feel free to swap, modify, or create your own version as you see fit. The italicized text suggests lengths for pauses. Adjust the pause lengths to your personal needs.

The bolded text is where you use the archetype in your day. You can also use the questions provided to do your own talk show in a group. Have fun with this. Give the archetypes time to talk to one another. It's amazing what insights they can share.

BEGIN SCRIPT

Get comfortable. Relax your body, starting at the head and working down to your toes. If you encounter stress or discomfort, massage it from your body. Put all stressful thoughts out of your mind, just for a little while. Slowly work your way through your body and release any tension you have. *(Pause for 1 or 2 minutes)*

Take a deep breath. On the exhale, slowly breathe out. Take a few moments to sit in the present. Feel your surroundings and whomever is sharing this journey with you. *(3 minutes)*

Imagine stepping outside this space into the woods beyond. You're walking away from civilization. Feel the ground beneath your feet and the cool, spring air on your face. Allow yourself to wander in whichever cardinal direction pleases you. *(3 minutes)*

As you continue wandering, you see the limbs and leaves of a giant oak tree. It appears near where you are. Walk over to this tree and examine it. Slowly work your way around the tree until you spot the outline of a doorway. It could be carved into the tree or simply be a hole inside it. When you have found it, reach out and touch the door. *(2 minutes)*

The door opens, exposing what appears to be a world beyond, another realm. You see the scene from your major arcana card. Step through this door and into a short tunnel that connects this world to that land. The tunnel appears as a hollow tube cut from the earth. It smells musty and rich in minerals. The tunnel guides you to the other side, a place outside of time. The land of tarot. You step across another doorway and find yourself standing in the major arcana card. *(3 mins)*

Visualize the card clearly. Use your senses to bring that card to life. Engage with this world. If there is a character on the card, interact with them. Listen to what they say, and note how they talk and move. Let them know that you want to embody the archetype, to become what it represents, to learn what it is like to be them. Spend time with this being, learning who it is and what they are. Become the person on that card. *(Long pause)*

When you are ready, allow that personality, that archetype to step into you. Open your eyes and become aware of the room we are in. One by one we'll introduce ourselves to the group and allow each other to share some knowledge about what it means to be the archetype of tarot.

Allow each archetype to interact with the others as if they were sitting on the stage of a talk show. Use the following questions as a guideline (you are also free to create your own):

How do you feel about one another?

What can the archetype teach the host or audience members?

What can you take back from meeting with us as people and as archetypes?

When you feel that all the archetypes have had their chance to speak their mind, guide the archetypes safely out of their hosts. This part is important to give the participants the space necessary to return to normal.

Close your eyes, and return to the land of tarot. Allow the archetype to leave your body and thank the personality for allowing them to work magic with us tonight. Do they have any parting thoughts or advice to share? If so, let them speak up now. *(3 minutes)*

Walk back through the world and reach the doorway you came through. Touch the door once more and allow it to show you the tunnel and our world once more. Walk back through the tunnel and step back into the woods you were in only a short while ago. *(1–2 mins)*

Make your way back to this house, to this room, and back into your body. When you are ready and feel safely returned inside your body, open your eyes. Welcome home. *(1–2 mins)*

END SCRIPT

Journaling Phase

When you are done using the script and the archetype, it's time to reflect on the experience. What gifts did your archetype share with you?

If you've done this with a group, have everyone discuss their experiences. Note that not everyone will want to share their thoughts; sometimes participants want to keep the experience to themselves, and this is perfectly fine. The Hermit, for example, may choose to keep what he learned to himself and reflect upon it further.

This exercise can be empowering and uplifting. Integrating archetypes into your personality can transform your life in many ways. After a few weeks of processing his experience, I had a student say this about the experience:

"The Hermit is the seeker, which is ironic I guess, but in a ways perhaps not, because who better to know when to stop seeking than the seeker? Well, he seems to know that anyway. I'm still learning that I don't have to continue seeking, that it might be unhealthy to do so. I'm also learning to let go of the past … because what was can sometimes hide what could be. In working with the Hermit, I found it easy to give myself permission to feel accepted for things that I normally would not have been."

Talking to Spiritual Entities

Tarot is an excellent tool to communicate with the unseen. There are many different ways to use your decks to speak to helpful entities. When you find yourself at a crossroads or at a loss as to what direction you need to move in, you can pull out your deck and ask for direction. One-card draws, spreads, and combining the cards with other devices like a pendulum can help you communicate with the unseen.

Before you can start having conversations with your guides, you need to know who you are talking to. Tarot can help you uncover identities. If you've worked with entities before, look through your deck to find a card to represent them. Court cards work great for guides who have a human form. You can pick one with qualities similar to how you recall them. Note the card and the name of the entity down in your journal so you don't forget.

If you're not sure who your guides are, use your deck to ask them to show you who they are. They may lead you to a card representing a personality trait, or a physical appearance.

In this section, we go over methods to use tarot as a communication tool for those entities. Spirit guides, entities, and higher powers surround us. These invisible presences play important roles in our lives. They provide us comfort and guidance, and they connect us to that divine pool which is greater than ourselves.

We know they're nearby and sometimes we cannot communicate with them. In these cases, tarot becomes a conduitthat gives them a way to communicate with you.

Exercise: Spread 'Em

This exercise gives you a taste of communicating with the spirits. It's the easiest way I know of receiving messages from our guides.

Grab your deck and think of an entity you wish to talk to. Call them to your side, ask them to be present with you. It sounds hokey but it works. If you have a question you'd like answered, ask them. Otherwise, you can ask them for any messages they may have.

When you are ready, shuffle your deck. Think about the spirit and invite them to use the tarot as their tool. Fan the cards out on the surface you're working on. Ask the guide to make the cards they want you to pick warmer. As you pass your hand over them, these warm spots are the cards you'll draw and use in the reading.

Pull those from the line up, turn them over, and proceed to interpret the message.

When you're done, thank the entity. Put the deck back together and shuffle once more.

EXERCISE: SPIRIT SPREAD

This three-card spread not only identifies who your guide is but gives them two ways to help you with your question or situation. Use the card before your guide's card, the card itself, and the card following to create a three-card reading.

The Spirit Spread Layout

Card one: The situation you want clarification on.

Card two: The guide. If you work with more than one guide, this card tells you who is answering the question. Use the information in the image to figure out how they'd help you move through the situation.

Card three: Your guide's advice. This card shows the next
step, a mental headspace, or insight into navigating the
situation smoothly.

For example:

The Tower represents the goddess Lilith. When I talk to
her and that card comes up, I know she's listening. When I
need specific advice from her, the Tower is the card to look for.

Next I shuffle my deck while focusing on her and her
energy. I speak my question out loud and then begin turning
cards over until the Tower shows up. The next card down is the
message from her. In this example, I drew the Six of Pentacles.
The message here tells me that I am making my own music
and learning how to grow and expand that so it affects the rest
of the world around me.

Using Pendulums

A pendulum is a weighted object suspended from a string,
chain, or wire. Today's pendulums are made by hanging crystals or metal weights from chains or strings. I have suspended
a key on a piece of string and used it just as accurately as a
store bought pendulum. When you hold the top of the string
between your fingers, the weight at the bottom swings back
and forth in equal directions.

Pendulums have been around for thousands of years. From
the eighteenth century on until the 1930s, they were used to
keep track of time, owing to how a pendulum's weight swings
from left to right in equal measure. They have also been used in

scientific instruments, and of course in spiritual practices like divination. The art of pendulum use as a divination device is known as cleidomancy. It works by reading energy patterns as it spins or swings from the string. Pendulums were used in the magic of ancient China to chase evil spirits away. They have also been used to find spots of concentrated energy.

Like any other divination tool, pendulums have their own language. When using your pendulum, hold the device between your second and middle fingers. Allow the weight at the end (crystal or key) to hang freely in the air. Learn to recognize what the "point" on your pendulum is. This is the lowest part of your pendulum where it focuses the energies and acts as a pointer. As the pendulum moves, it will swing in various patterns. This is how it talks to you.

When holding the tool, keep your arm still and relaxed, not stiff. Allow the pendulum to sway by itself. To stop the weight's movement use the hand not holding the pendulum to make the object stop. Before you can successfully use your pendulum, you need to attune it first. Attuning your pendulum acclimates it to your energy. It also allows the pendulum to show you what yes, no, or maybe means.

Attuning the Pendulum: Pick up and hold your pendulum. While the pendulum sways, ask it to work on behalf of your highest self. Continue to let the pendulum swing and soak up your energy. After a while, stop it with your other hand. It is now attuned to you.

Discovering yes: Pick up and hold your pendulum. Tell the pendulum to "Show me a positive gesture." Pull your hand off the pointer, and let the pointer swing. Watch the pointer sway in for a few minutes. The direction it moves in is your positive response. Thank the pendulum for giving you an answer. Stop the pointer. I recommend you write the direction down on a piece of paper. Repeat this process once to confirm that this is the positive movement. If the pendulum gives you a different response re-attune the pendulum.

Discovering no: Pick up and hold your pendulum. Tell the pendulum to "Show me a negative gesture." Pull your hand off the pointer, and let the it swing. Watch the pointer sway in for a few minutes. The direction it moves in is your negative response. Thank the pendulum for giving you an answer. Stop the pointer. I recommend you write the direction down on a piece of paper. Repeat this process once to confirm that this is the negative movement. If the pendulum gives you a different response re-attune the pendulum.

You can also uncover other responses and other movements as you build a relationship. Pendulums, like tarot decks, can develop a personality. Sometimes if you ask your pendulum too many questions or the same question over and over again, they'll give you a snarky response, or a confusing response. I've found that if I ask my pendulum to "show me what a gesture means" more than once, I get a completely different response. It's as if the device is telling me to trust the first two swings and stop asking it to repeat itself. Treat your pendulum with respect and never abuse it.

Sometimes tarot isn't the best tool to work with your guides, so it's good to remember that pendulums and tarot work beautifully together. Perhaps a card's personality doesn't jive with the cards, or maybe an additional item to help focus the message is needed. When you use the two devices together, start small. Don't use all the cards, just start with the major arcana. In fact, use only the majors with the following exercises and see what big picture items your guides can help you with.

EXERCISE: WHO AM I TALKING TO?

This first exercise gives you practice on learning who you are talking to. This exercise may take some time, but it's important—it gives your spirit guides the chance to pick out their own personal archetype.

For example, if you considered your grandfather a teacher or mentor and he appears to want to speak, he may choose the Hierophant card to tell you that it's him and not your grandmother, who may be seen as the Empress.

Break out the major arcana cards from your deck. Put these into a Majors Matrix.

Hold your pendulum in the usual way and ask the entity to use the pendulum for communicating. Tell the entity to move the pendulum in the positive motion. Once your pendulum moves in the affirmative motion, you can stop the pendulum. Thank the entity for giving you a response.

Hover the pendulum over the Fool card and ask the entity, "Do you see yourself as this archetype?"

You'll be doing this over all twenty-two cards. It seems like a long process but it's worth it, as we're giving the entity a chance to select a single card to represent them.

Patience is key here. Wait until the pendulum moves, positively or negatively. If you get a negative moment, take the card out of the matrix and move onto the next. Repeat the question until you get a positive answer.

When you do get a positive motion, spend some time with that card. Think about all the people and spiritual entities in your life that share the archetype represented by the card. Write up a list of names. Then pull out the pendulum once more and using your list, ask the entity if their name is on the list. If it's a yes, then go down the list and read off each name until the entity gives you a name. If the entity tells you that it is not on the list, then you might want to find a trusted spirit medium and see if they can help you uncover who this guide is, or spend some time in meditation and figure out who is trying to guide you.

When you are done with this process, thank both the pendulum and the guide for their insight. Put the pendulum back in its case for safe-keeping.

Exercise: What Action Should I Take?

Guides love talking. You can turn to them when you need advice on the projects you're working on.

Shuffle your tarot deck (you can use all seventy-eight cards or just the majors for this exercise) and allow your spirit guide to pick cards that represent actions or energies that you should focus on learning at any particular moment.

When you are ready, spread the deck out in a line. It's okay if some cards overlap. You can use the pendulum to isolate single cards as you need them. Raise your pendulum up over the length of the cards. Ask your guide to use the pendulum to focus over the cards that can help you in your project. The more specific you can be, the more specific and focused the cards can get about the situations you face yourself in.

Allow the pendulum to sway naturally. Look closely at the direction in which the pendulum moves. Pick up those cards. Focus your attention on these cards. Spread them out and repeat the process until the pendulum isolates one card. It's okay if you have more than one card at the end; it may mean there are a few steps to focus on before the project is done.

Examine the cards and think about what they mean to you. You can also perform a reading with these cards and figure out what the answer you receive means for you.

When you are done with this process, thank both the pendulum and the guide for their insight. Put the pendulum back in its case for safe keeping.

EXERCISE: YES OR NO

Get out your deck and look at the cards face up. Locate two cards that represent yes and no for you. Put them on the table face-up next to each other.

Hold your pendulum in between the two cards. Ask the pendulum a yes or no question and wait until the pendulum begins to move. If it moves towards the positive card, then your answer is yes. If it moves to your negative card, your answer is no. If it does not gravitate towards either card, it may not know the answer or you may be asking the wrong question. At this point, you can ask the pendulum if it does know the answer, or you can work with the tarot alone to figure out what needs to be done next.

When you are done with this process, thank both the pendulum and the guide for their insight. Put the pendulum back in its case for safe keeping.

A note on silly questions: As you'll see in the example below, you could use this method to ask questions that are a little more light-hearted. Just as your tarot deck has a personality, the pendulum and your guides also have personalities. While asking silly questions can be fun, don't do it too often or your guides and the tools won't take your requests seriously when you need them to.

For example:

I use the Magician (a positive force of manifestation in my life) as my "yes" card, and the Tower (representative of the kind of energy I try avoid having too much of in my life) as my "no" card. I set them down in front of me, face up, and leave some space in-between the cards. Then I pick up my pendulum and hold it.

I've decided to ask the cards whether or not I should spend $1,500 on buying all the books on my wish list. It's a totally self-indulgent question. So I hold my pendulum and ask my guides whether or not to spend the money.

The pendulum takes a long while to give me an answer. I apologize to my guides and let them know I don't think it's an appropriate question to ask them, but it *is* something fun to ask while writing this book. They tell me no. I note this information down in my journal, shuffle the cards, and carefully put my pendulum back in its case.

For further study and reflection on the topics included in this chapter, look for the following books:

Davich, Victor. *8 Minute Meditation*. New York: Penguin, 2004.

Galenorn, Yasmine. *Tarot Journeys: Adventures in Self-Transformation*. Kirkland, WA: Nightqueen Enterprises, 2016.

Heidrick, Bill. "Tarot Meditations 1975–76." http://hermetic.com/heidrick/Tarot_meditations .html. (Includes meditations based off the teachings of Paul Foster Case.)

Morgan, Michele. *A Magical Course in Tarot: Reading the Cards in a Whole New Way.* Berkeley, CA: Conari Press, 2002.

Powell, Robert, trans. *Meditations on the Tarot: A Journey into Christian Hermeticism.* New York: Penguin Group, 1985.

Webster, Richard. *Pendulum Magic for Beginners.* Woodbury, MN: Llewellyn Publications, 2011.

Chapter 7

Invocations for
Transformation

Manifest Your Desires with Tarot

By the end of this chapter you'll:

- Understand the components of invocation

- Read and use pre-created invocations to
  understand their power

- Create situational-based tarot invocations
  to attract a better life

- Use tarot to determine the outcome of an
  invocation

Before we jump right into the heart of this chapter, I want
to take a moment to discuss a few terms. These words are

"spell" and "prayer." These charged, polarized words evoke strong reactions when spoken. They are also two methods of manifesting desires and making connections in your life. *Tarot Inspired Life* is an inclusive work. The lessons mentioned in this chapter, and in the next chapter on ceremonies, can be adapted to suit your life and the wondrous events your spiritual path holds. With this in mind, I'm not using the terms "spell" or "prayer." Instead, this chapter uses the neutral designation of invocation to strike a harmonious balance.

Simply put, an invocation is a spoken, written, or gestured expression that sparks, influences, or creates a petition to the divine forces to act and help out on your behalf. Anyone can use invocations. Faith in, and the use of, invocations are universal and have been an integral part of spiritual practices over the development of cultures worldwide. At minimum, all you need to do a successful invocation is the desire to better your life and the will to manifest it. Adding ingredients like tarot cards to an invocation helps ensure the outcome swings in your favor.

People have been performing invocations for millennia now—sometimes without even knowing it. Any time you've asked for help, blessed someone, or sent positive thoughts of health, luck, or happiness to someone, you've sent out an invocation. Purposes for invocations are limitless and include: healing, love, money, success, fertility, longevity, and protection from disaster, ill fortune, or evil. You can direct them towards yourself or someone else. Use invocations to protect yourself from external forces such as spirits and ghosts. When you combine the power of invocation with tarot, you can use the cards as foci for your desires.

In this chapter we'll explore the power of invocations and the ways to manifest your heart's desire. Tarot is a symbolic language we can use to communicate your desires symbolically with the divine on your behalf. You can find many books in the stores with pre-created invocations (in this case, they're spell books). My goal for this chapter is to help guide you into creating your own personalized invocations.

Introduction to Tarot Invocations

I highly recommend picking and dedicating a deck for use exclusively with this sort of spiritual work. Sometimes casting invocations requires you to keep several cards out for many days, weeks, or months. If you have only one deck and your invocation requires five cards to remain separate from your deck for seven days, you'll be missing those cards when you go to read for yourself or others. In fact, the more you use the tarot for invocations or ritual use, the more decks you may want to have. In the past, I have cast up to three invocations working in tandem to achieve a singular goal.

There's no hard and fast rules to getting a second deck. You can pick a completely different deck or buy another copy of a favorite. Size doesn't matter, but there are benefits for each type: small, large, or digital. Tiny cards require less space to spread out. They can be hidden from prying eyes in boxes or in books. Stand larger cards up where you can easily see them as a reminder of what goal you are working for. Digital cards (i.e., smartphone apps) allow you to take your invocations wherever you go.

You'll need a suitable location to lay out your invocations. Often you can use a table top or a shelf where the cards can sit and be left untroubled. I use a dedicated shelf to place my invocations. For those who may not have a general space to keep a spread out or who have roommates who may not agree with what you're doing, I suggest converting a dresser drawer in which to keep your invocations. This way, the spread is out of the way and isn't causing strife with others.

The key to crafting successful tarot invocations is two-fold; the first part is getting to know your cards intimately. Understand what each image means to you personally. Know the symbols, colors, numbers, and how each card resonates with you. This is where part one comes into play. Remember your tarot PDA? It's time to break it out. You want the deck to become an extension of who you are and how you feel. You *could* just use book definitions, but they may not define what you personally associate with a card at that moment.

Invocations, like tarot readings, are intimate. They use your energy, ideas, and your connections. The more you learn about yourself and how you feel and associate to the cards in the deck, the deeper and more available the energies you'll need for casting an invocation can become. For example, when you create an invocation for love, you may want to factor in the following items: what that person looks like, how you want them to express their feelings, and what symbols you associate with love. Deciding on each factor can mean the difference between selecting the Lovers card (personally, a good choice for a short term relationship) and the Two of Cups (a longer, deeply connected relationship). Additionally, any cards containing those symbols you identify with love (hearts, roses, or certain colors) can also help focus your goal and sway the invocation's outcome.

The next important part of successfully crafting tarot invocations is being specific in your requests. Asking the universe to "send love" is too general. What sort of love do you wish to draw to yourself? Do you want to work on loving yourself? Do you want to attract a certain person to you? Or perhaps you desire to craft a love invocation to raise love energy so everyone on Earth feels a boost.

Doing an invocation for any of those above examples requires different cards and symbols. Some may contain the same cards but their end results yield different effects. In fact, if you were to cast a tarot invocation for each of those questions, the cards, feelings, and vibes sent out would yield three different effects.

Unlike tarot spreads, invocations follow no real structure. They could be as simple as lighting a candle and silently asking your deity to help you while holding a card in your hand. Other invocations are more elaborate and take time to set up, resolve, and work their way into your life. I personally prefer the less-is-more approach. Just as I dislike spreads that use more than twelve cards, I try to keep my invocations limited in card quantity, usually no more than six to help focus the intent.

Sample Tarot Invocations

If you're unsure what I mean by tarot invocations, I've added a few sample invocations to give you an idea of what they can look like. Treat them as recipes to help you create additions or variations for your life.

If you decide to use one of the following invocations, don't use them as written. They are based on my personal card meanings and symbolic connections. Read the rest of this chapter before testing these invocations out. The details here will help you understand how they were constructed and how you can modify them to fit your personal needs. Personalizing your invocations will give your petition more power and energy. It may make the outcome more achievable.

Addiction-Breaking Invocation

Use this invocation to help break addiction. Whether it be food, cigarettes, alcohol, or the internet, breaking an addiction is a hard but worthwhile goal. Speak to your doctor before you begin this work so they can monitor your health when doing this.

Intent: Envision yourself as you want to be—healthy, whole, and free of the addictive substance or item. Imagine the new goals and activities you can replace the addictive habit with. Know you live a clean life and note what it looks like. Include your family and friends who cheer you on.

When you are ready, name your addiction and write it down on paper. Also write down what you're replacing it with.

Other required components:

- The Devil: Represents the addictive substance

- Temperance: Represents the balance to restore in your body and life

- Strength: Reminds you of the internal courage and ability to break your addictions. It's going to be hard but you can do this.

- Ten of Cups: Represents your free and clean life

- Safe addiction-free environment: Before you begin this invocation, clear your space of any temptations. If you have a medically prescribed plan, make sure that you have all the tools you need to ensure success.

- Cheerleaders: giving up bad habits you've been doing for so long is hard. Gather your friends and let them support you as you need.

- An image of your addiction(s). You'll be cutting this image during the invocation.

- String

- Scissors

Activity: Place the Devil from your deck in front of you. This card represents your addiction. Tie an image of the addiction to the Devil using the string. Imagine the voice of the addiction calling out to you, luring you in. Don't give in—for now, I want you to understand the cravings.

When you have a sense of what those cravings feel like, take the piece of paper used to write your intention and set it on top of the Devil card. Say your intention out loud with conviction three times.

Pick up the Strength card. Think about how strong you are. You can do this! Your addiction has no power over you. Strength is you and your cheerleaders.

Place Strength over the Devil. Tell the Devil how you don't need it anymore. When you feel the cravings, hold Strength and remind yourself that you *can* beat this addiction. You are stronger. Let the Strength card become a talisman.

Remove the Strength card and set it aside. Pick up Temperance and place it on top of the Devil. This card will remain on the Devil until you have a better sense of balance and control over your ability to stay away from the addiction. It also blocks you from physically seeing the addiction.

Place the Ten of Cups over the Temperance card. Think about your future addiction-free self and how good it feels to have gotten rid of the Devil and its power. Your new life is stronger and more balanced now.

Take the string and tie this three-card bundle together. Find a place in your house where it can be left undisturbed as you work through the addiction. Carry the Strength card with you as a reminder of how strong you are and how you can overcome the voice of addiction.

When you have broken the addiction, cut the string loose from the bundle and the string holding your addiction to the Devil. Cleanse the cards before returning them to the deck. (I suggest smudging.) Cut, bury, or burn the picture of your addiction as an offering, and thank your divine helpers for their aid.

Self-Love Invocation

Use this invocation when you feel down about yourself, whether it's your looks, weight, or health. Its aim is to boost your spirits and remind you that you are perfect the way you are.

Intent: "I am lovable. There is no one in the universe like me. I am unique. This is who I am, mind, body, and spirit."

Items Needed:

- The Lovers. Love and affection is a birthright. Have respect for who you are and what you look like.

- A photo of yourself that you like, or a photocopy of it

- A mirror

- Colored paper in the shade you identify with love

- Scissors and glue

Activity: Be alone when you doing this invocation. While holding a mirror (or standing in front of a full-length mirror naked), look at yourself. Look at your body's curves and wrinkles. Look into your own eyes. This is you, and there is no one who exists quite like you. Keep this image of yourself in your mind, for it wants love, it deserves love, and this invocation will give it some love.

Hold the photo of yourself at arm's length. Think about how that picture makes you feel and then transfer that feeling to the image of you reflected in the mirror. The mirror reflection is just like the photo and deserves the same love and respect.

Say this out loud three times, "I am unique in the universe. There is no one like me anywhere." Connect to the feelings of love and happiness you feel when around a loved one. Send this energy out into the universe so it knows you are capable of love and want more self-love in return.

Pick up the colored paper. Cut out a heart large enough for you to glue the picture and tuck the Lovers card onto it. The heart, like you, is the perfect shape as is. While thinking about love and how special and unique you are to deserve that love, glue the photograph or a photocopy of it onto the card.

Think about the symbolism of creating and giving a heart to yourself and how that feels to you. You are unique and deserve the love you can give yourself.

Tuck the Lovers card next to your photo.

Hold the finished valentine close to your heart. This is a present and a gift you give to yourself. Find a place of honor in your home to display your gift. Look at it often as a reminder of how worthy of love you are.

Invocations like this don't necessarily need to end, but if you decide to end it, gently dispose of the heart by recycling it as an offering to yourself. Cleanse the card before returning it to the deck. Thank your divine helpers for their aid.

Four Steps to a Successful Invocation

Invocations have four steps:

1. Visualizing the outcome

2. Crafting a statement of intent to achieve your goal

3. Selecting components to aid your petition (components are words, statements, goodies, or sounds)

4. Releasing the intent into the world with energy

All these elements help focus our mental image of the goal, our identification with it, the repetition of our intent to achieve this goal, and projection of our will. It becomes our petition to the spirits, deities, or the divine force for their aid so that we can achieve the desired outcome.

In the next sections, we'll tackle how invocations are put together. I'll define each step and provide an example of the invocation from start to finish. It's my hope that when you finish the end of this section you'll have the basics down to craft and attempt some of your own.

Visualize the Outcome

The first step in casting a successful invocation is to visualize the outcome of your invocation. This is what Stephen Covey calls "starting with the end in mind." Before you can ask the universe, spirits, and deities out there to deliver the life you desire, you first need to picture what it looks like.

Visualizing your invocation's outcome is easy to do, requiring the best of daydreaming and playing the What If game to help you build concrete snippets of what your desired life looks like. At this step, you use your mind's eye and internal camera to take a snapshot of what you envision your life to be after the invocation has come true. Make it as real as you can so that if you told someone about it, they would exclaim, "Aha, I see what you want!"

Sometimes this picture is simple, especially if the outcome is to bring an item into your life. Do you want a new phone? How about a new car? Go to the web and print out an image and the item's specs. What if the outcome is a new house, job, lover, or losing weight? You can't just search the internet, print the solution out, and hope to get it. When it comes to the less concrete invocations, creativity is your friend. Write, draw, or otherwise create various possibilities of the shape of the outcome.

Let's say you want a new place to live. Homes define us, make us feel comfortable and supported, give us a place to store our items, and allow us to build a life. You could just stand up where you are, toss your hands to the sky and call out, "Please help me find a new home," but nothing in this statement describes what your ideal home is. If the universe delivered a place to you, with this wording, it'd be in a "take it or leave it" gesture.

You know you have preferences, likes, and dislikes, so take time to think about your outcome. What does home look like? Are you asking to buy a single family detached house? Maybe all you want is a new apartment in a location you desire? Where is this home—in the city, suburbs, or completely out of the state you are living in? How much square footage should it have? How much money do you want to spend on rent/mortgage? All of these questions are important to the outcome of finding the home that is right for you.

Exercise: Visualizing the Outcome

Use this exercise to practice generating specific outcomes. Think about areas you'd love to improve in your life. Would you like a new house? A new job? A new tablet? Perhaps, you'd like to to bring creativity or energy into your life. No matter what you choose, the steps to reaching those goals are the same.

First, make your list of desires.

Pick an item off the list to use throughout this chapter. Daydream and think about how this choice improves your life. See yourself at the new job. See yourself driving that new car. See yourself free from smoking. See yourself and the goal so clearly in your mind. Make it real.

Once you have a clear and detailed picture of exactly what you want out of the invocation, move on to the next step, which is crafting a statement for that goal.

Crafting Your Statement of Intent

The second step to casting a successful invocation is crafting your goal's statement. Take your visualization and write it out. Your statement of intent, along with any of the components your invocation has, is the fuel to drive the desire behind getting what you want.

Take time to craft this statement. Words have weight and power behind them. When you tell someone you love them, they receive the feeling of being important. When you are angry and yell at a puppy, the animal senses your anger and feels hurt. Therefore it's important to think about the words your statement contains. The clearer you can be about what your intended outcome is, the easier the divine can give it to you.

Artists can use this time to draw or collage what is desired. Pictures are worth more than a thousand words, so show the divine what you want. The more specific you are in creating your new life image, the easier it is for the universal energies to deliver it to you.

Exercise: Crafting a Statement

We'll use the visualization from your last exercise and transform it into words that you'll speak and turn into energy. You don't need to craft perfect sentences; my invocation statements get messy while working on them. I worry about leaving out key details, so I tend to add too many sometimes. Write and revise what you put on paper so you have a detailed statement to use during the casting stage.

There are no hard and fast rules for crafting a good statement. Here's what works for me:

- Write in the present tense. Being in the present not only strengthens our connection to the desire but it also enforces the idea we already have it.

- Be positive. Remember, this outcome is beneficial for your life. Be positive and show excitement.

- Write from your heart. Rhyming and poems are great, but if you're not a poet, don't write in verse.

- Be specific. Add as many concrete details to make your goal as real as possible.

For example:

When my partner and I moved across town, we had a long list of items we wanted for our new sanctuary. Here's our brain dump of what we wanted:

The perfect home for us is in Portland, Oregon, located somewhere in the southwest quadrant. One story, no more than 1500 square feet. Three bedrooms, two bathrooms. Near public transportation, access to grocery stores within walking distance. The neighborhood is quiet and well established, with friendly neighbors who talk to one another. NO HOA. Two-car garage for our cars and motorcycle. Lots of trees—we want to feel like we're living in the forest. Easy maintenance yard, less grass. Our mortgage is no more than $1500. We want a home to call sanctuary. It's also got a good internet connection through DSL or cable modem.

Once you've written a clear statement of intent, move on to the next step: selecting components to boost the energy.

Selecting Components to Aid Your Petition

Let's go shopping! This is where you select ingredients with symbolic connections to the outcome you desire: tarot cards, crystals, pictures, plants, oils, or other items else you have nearby. Physical objects have energy. These items and their energy are the code to unlocking the specific outcome you desire.

Using components gives your petition a special boost of energy. Putting all these items with their similar vibes together focuses your intent and aids the divine in finding exactly what you want.

When I cast invocations, I look through my deck for cards with vibes, colors, and symbolism connecting the goal. Doing so reinforces my desire. It tells the universe how strongly I want to draw my desires in my life. I look at external factors such as the day of the week, the season, and moon phase to give me the upper hand as well.

Some components you'll select intuitively or "just because." Others you'll learn about over time and from other resources, like almanacs. But when you coordinate your invocations around days that have a like-minded energy to your outcome, every little bit helps.

Exercise: Picking Components

Look through your invocation deck for images and cards with sympathetic energies to your desires. If your goal is to manifest a long and lasting love, look for a card that shows two loving individuals. If you want cash, look for a corresponding card that represents money gain to you.

Don't limit yourself to just cards either. I've used magazine images, herbs, plants, crystals, stuffed animals, incense, and photographs for various invocations in my life. Let your creativity run wild.

Also pick the date to release your intention. You can choose any date you want, but like I said, some dates are more harmonious than others. Pick a date that holds meaning to you and one on which you know you'll have time alone.

Grab all the sympathetic items you think may help your petition and place them in a single location. When you're ready to release your intent, all your tools will be in one spot, which helps simplify the process.

For example:

My friend Andy wants a new job. Andy gathers the following components: a hand-drawn image of a check with his name on it and how much the company will pay him for his services during each pay period. He also includes the Eight of Pentacles, the Three of Pentacles, and the Ten of Pentacles. He puts everything into a green envelope and tucks this envelope into his portfolio.

Have you finished selecting your components and cards? Move on to the final step, which is to release your intent into the universe.

Releasing the Intent and Energy into the World

The final step to a successful invocation is releasing the intent and energy to the world so it can start searching on your behalf. This energy is the kinetic force setting an invocation in motion. It is an active thought or physical action telling the universe "get going and don't come back until you find it."

As for how to do it, it can be as easy as sitting in front of a candle, holding an image of the car of your dreams, and saying out loud "I own a new car by September." You then offer the statement, components, and desire up while continuing to put money in your savings account to buy the car in the desired month and year.

You can also turn this moment into a more elaborate ceremony where you meditate and focus on what you want, hold the cards, dance, toss glitter, and then release the energies to work their own magic. However, time is precious, so I like to keep my intensions direct and simple.

No matter how you set your petition into motion, stating your intent gives your invocation the spark it needs to move forward. You command the universe and direct energies to work on your behalf. Once you release, your job is done. Have faith and know these forces are working on your behalf to help you attain what you released.

Experiment and play with different types of invocations, components, and words to say. Keep clear records in your tarot journal—record dates and other information to help you either recreate a successful invocation or retool it if your ceremony fizzles out and doesn't happen the way you hoped. Keep doing this over and over until your system works for you.

EXERCISE: RELEASING THE INTENT AND ENERGY INTO THE UNIVERSE

Make sure you are undisturbed when you begin releasing your intent. Turn off your devices, keep music to a minimum (unless music is a component of your invocation), and tell the housemates to leave you alone for a bit.

Gather your components. If you followed my advice, they should be ready in one place.

Arrange the components as you desire. This is a subjective step. This is also where experimentation comes into play. Take notes (or pictures) on your arrangements. If you need examples, you can go back to the Sample Tarot Invocations section. Look at the sections marked "Activity," as they correspond to this step.

Get comfortable. Go back to your first visualization. Hold the outcome clearly in your mind and feel it. When you are ready, speak your intention out loud—this part is important). Direct it out into the universe. Let the universe know you've gathered all these items and pulled them together so they can help bring the outcome to you.

Light any candles, dance, drum, or make actions you know to help boost the signal and make the unknown forces work together.

After you feel that you have released enough energy, move the invocation items out of the way and into a place they can sit undisturbed. This is the part where you leave these items alone and let the divine do what it does to bring your goal to you.

Post-Invocation Care

As I mentioned, some invocations require you to keep the cards laid out for an indefinite period of time. There's no hard and fast rule for the length, however. In fact, you define "indefinite period of time." I find the best way to know when an invocation works is when you have the desired outcome. So while the invocation is doing what it needs to do to promote what you desire, leave the components where they are (or take it with you, if your invocation is portable).

After you release your intent into the hands of the divine, your job is done. Let the unseen forces of spirituality work on your behalf without interference. Let the invocation process unfold naturally. When I step aside and allow the situation to happen on its own, the goal comes to me when it needs to—not sooner or later. It's not easy to do, but trust is a necessary step.

Once you have received the invocation's outcome, there is one more step you need to do: dismantle the invocation and properly dispose of any components. Burn, recycle, or trash any components.

Reintegrate any used tarot cards back into the deck. I like to shuffle them back into their deck and store them in their box. If you don't think this is adequate to clear the energies put into the invocation, use incense or a smudge stick to clear any remaining energies before returning the cards back to the deck and their home.

That's it. Nothing fancy. Just clean up after yourself.

Dressing Up Your Invocations

Invocations take many forms and shapes. The simplest tarot invocation is to lay cards down somewhere in a pile. Sometimes, dressing up your invocation aids in the outcome of your petition. It's also just fun to do. Putting happy energy into an invocation may attract helpers to attain the goal for you. The following are some of my favorite ways to dress my invocations up:

Create a Mojo Bag

Sometimes you'll want to carry a spell with you but using a spread and a pack of cards might be too much. In this case, make a sachet (or mojo bag) to carry your intention around. Grab an organza bag and place cards into the bag. Then you can add any flowers, stones, or herbs with it.

Design a Mandala

Mandalas are spiritual pictures taking specific forms. If your invocation requires a lot of cards, place them in some sort of meaningful pattern, Then adorn the image with other spell components such as rice, shells, coins, and so on.

Place Invocations in an Envelope

Put your invocations inside an envelope large enough to hold your cards. You can carry the envelope around with you.

Was the Tarot Invocation Successful?

Ideally you know when an invocation works because you have gained the item or outcome you set out to achieve. However, success isn't as clear cut, especially when months or years have passed and you cannot recall what the invocation was done for in the first place. (This is another reason why writing about your experience is so important.)

Turn to tarot to know when your invocation was a success. You can also use this spread before doing the invocation to receive advice on how to fine tune your invocation, as well as give you information you may need before casting.

The Tarot Invocation Layout

Card One: Is my invocation's intent true? What is the real reason behind doing this invocation?

Card Two: What, if any, am I missing from the invocation?

Card Three: What is the outcome if I do this invocation now?

Card Four (optional, based on the satisfaction of the last question): If now is not the time, what do I need to do to bring a better time about?

Shuffle your cards and do the spread. If the answers are satisfactory, move ahead with your invocation. If the answers aren't satisfactory or you're not sure when to do the invocation, continue to refine your invocation. Redo the spread another day.

For further study and reflection on the topics included in this chapter, look for the following books:

Dominguez Jr., Ivo. *Casting Sacred Space: The Core of All Magickal Work*. San Francisco: Red Wheel/Weiser, 2012.

Graham, Sasha. *365 Tarot Spells: Creating the Magic in Each Day*. Woodbury, MN: Llewellyn Publications, 2016.

Morrison, Dorothy. *Everyday Tarot Magic: Meditation & Spells.* St. Paul, MN: Llewellyn Publications, 2002.

Pamita, Madame. *Madame Pamita's Magical Tarot: Using the Cards to Make Your Dreams Come True.* Newburyport, MA: Red Wheel/Weiser, 2018.

Renee, Janina. *Tarot Spells.* St. Paul, MN: Llewellyn Publications, 1990.

Tyson, Donald. *Portable Magic: Tarot Is the Only Tool You Need.* St. Paul, MN: Llewellyn Publications. 2006.

Chapter 8

Rituals for Transformation
Manifest Your Tarot Inspired Life

By the end of this chapter you'll:

- Understand the power of ritual

- Create a personalized area for tarot rituals

- Create and experience rituals to honor nature's cycles (or adapt these to other personal cycles)

- Use tarot to craft year-long life changing/affirming rituals

A woman lights a blue candle sitting next to her writing desk. She bows her head and silently whispers a few words, inviting her creative muse to come and meet her at the desk.

She pulls the chair out, sits down, and stares at a blank page on her computer. She inhales deeply to clear her mind. Then she reaches out and sets her timer for twenty-five minutes. As the timer ticks, she pulls the keyboard close. The woman's muse inspires her and she begins to type.

The above illustrates a simple writing ritual I've done to meet the muse at the page. Contrary to popular belief, people love building rituals into their daily lives.

Simply stated, a ritual is a symbolic action people do for a specific purpose. Rituals set intention and give us space for achieving our goals. Many people think rituals are bound within religious context, but this isn't true. Waking up in the morning and preparing for the day—getting dressed, grabbing coffee, heading to work—that's a ritual. In this case, you're using those steps to prepare yourself from being asleep to being awake and ready head to the office. Bedtime routines are also rituals, easing us from being awake to getting the proper amount of rest.

Rituals ease the transition from being in one state of mind to another by clearing room in both our heads and the physical realm. In a way, rituals become triggers our minds and bodies use. Transitions are important. They help us ease into experiencing various life events.

Rituals help us learn new habits or knowledge. They take us from an unawake state to a higher awareness where we can focus our mind and be open to new ideas and thought patterns.

When we create rituals, we show the divine we're willing to meet it at its level and expand our understanding of the world.

You can adapt ritual to fit any aspect of your life. Rituals can be as simple as taking the first five minutes of your waking day to think about what appointments you have, or they can be as elaborate as an hour-long process where you invoke deity and guides in receiving messages. Rituals help you honor and deepen the connection you have in your spiritual practice. They can help reconnect you to nature and your personal rhythms and help support your visions for the future.

Rituals are powerful. When you are in ritual space, you think differently. You see the world differently, and you use your brain to make new connections. Ideas flow naturally and brainstorms become second nature. Rituals have the potential to help you accomplish goals and dreams and seek out new endeavors due to their ability to alter your mind.

In this chapter, I'll guide you through creating rituals and applying them in your life. Create a special space to honor and perform rituals. You'll start integrating daily, monthly, and seasonal rituals into your practice. Then I'll introduce you to a year-long tarot ritual with the potential to change your life and give you what you need to learn to advance yourself as you grow in life.

Setting the Stage for Ritual

Before we create and work with rituals, we need to do some preparation first. Prepping for ritual has three parts: finding a space to do the work, decorating the space to support your intent, and making a focus (in this case, an altar to hold your cards). The next two sections walk you through locating a special space to work your magic and designing an area to store the rituals so that nothing interferes with the cards and the energy you are raising.

Setting Space

There's one action I do in my life (and in ritual space) to help me prepare for the work I do—I arrange my house in certain ways to allow various goals to unfold. It doesn't matter how big or small the physical area is. For example, my writing space takes up a small corner of one room. Conversely, my reading space fills up an entire room. I honor each area the same.

I'm talking about setting space here. It's important, so important it has two definitions. Setting space, in the first sense, is to physically designate an area specific to a task. In this case, it's about finding a location in your home to keep your tarot rituals. Setting space is also a practice where we dress the area with our energy. You can do this with your voice, dancing, clapping, or other ways while imbuing the air within this location with a specific intention.

No two tasks or jobs are created equal, so when we go to set about psyching ourselves up for staying on task, we need to have the right location and elements to make sure the work we do can be done at our ability's peak. We don't eat in the same place we sleep because sleeping requires different items. Likewise, our brains need to be in different modes for us to tackle different tasks.

When I set the space for reading cards, I do several things beforehand: I make sure the table and chairs are out, I place a table cloth onto the table to give me a canvas to lay cards down and also protect my cards from residue, and I place the deck and any other table dressings on the cloth. Before I am ready to receive my first client, I dress the energy of the room by walking around the table to honor the ten directions. I also send out a prayer of intention that aligns what I do with what I hope to receive in return. I also spritz a bit of Florida Water in the air to align my senses with the desire to provide quality spiritual advice in exchange for payment and my client's willingness to be open to our time together.

From this example, setting space encompasses both the inner and outer worlds. By bringing out my tools and decorating the space, my mind and body get alerted to the task at hand. I dress the air and the energetic space by aligning the directions to my intentions. This activity trains my mind to step away from the endless chatter from my monkey mind so I can be present and ready to focus on my clients. The spritz of Florida Water smells nice and triggers a magical vibe reminding me of my sacred duty to read responsibly. It's the final trick I use to take my mind from the everyday headspace to my reader headspace.

Your Tarot Altar

Once you've found a space for doing rituals, its time to create an altar. An altar is a focused flat space which houses the items needed to perform specific goals. Your tarot altar is a place where you can lay down and keep track of rituals done with your cards.

Get creative with the location. While using a shelf, a fireplace mantle, or a table are great locations, they are highly visible and susceptible to curious pets. I have a friend who put her altar inside a drawer of her dresser. Doing so gives her the space she needs for her practices, protects the space from pets, and keeps snooping roommates from disturbing her practice. She also keeps her decks inside this drawer.

You can designate furniture as your altar. I used to have a three-tiered shelf system. The shelves held my tools, working invocations, and other items necessary for my spiritual practice.

There is no correct way to make an altar. It can be a small and portable item you carry with you, or it can take up the entire space in a whole room. Use what you have. The more you practice rituals, the more your altar locations will evolve. I've gone from a three-tier shelf system to several shelves in various bookcases, closet drawers, and now even my desk contains ritual space.

EXERCISE: SETTING YOUR TAROT ALTAR SPACE

Use this exercise as your first dip into ritual. It works best if you have already found the place you'll designate for performing rituals. If you haven't found a proper location, apply the steps in this exercise to other areas of your life. Before you begin, you'll need a rattle, drum, or some noise maker. If you don't have an item to make a beat, use your voice or hands to make some sound.

Setting space can be as easy as closing your eyes and inviting the muse to come in and play. It can be a simple declaration of what you plan on doing in the next twenty-five minutes, the next hour, or during the day. Learn some techniques and then decide on how you want to set space. No matter what you decide, designate this space as a safe one where you can experiment and grow.

I want you to try the ten-point circle method of setting space. This barebones outline can be adapted to fit your needs. The first action I do before working on anything is to "dress" the space with the intention. My intention is the goal, feeling, or outcome I'd like to see during the time I'm focusing in on that place. Take a few moments to think of the feeling you want your space to contain.

The next activity I do is to cast a ten-point circle. This technique, taught to me by Shon Clark, helps gather the energies of each direction and gets my head focused on what I want to do. The steps of the ten-point circle are easy:

1. Face east and honor the energies of the east. For me this is the rising sun, air, and the suit of swords. When you're done, thank the energies for being present in your life and move

clockwise to the south. Clap or chant as you shift locations.

2. Face south and honor the energies of the south. For the this is the midday sun at its warmest, fire; and the suit of wands. When you're done, thank the energies for being present in your life and move clockwise to the west. Clap or chant as you shift locations.

3. Face west and honor the energies of the west. For me this is the setting sun, water, and the suit of cups. When you're done, thank the energies for being present in your life and move clockwise to the north. Clap or chant as you shift locations.

4. Face north and honor the energies of the north. For me this is the darkened sky, earth, and the suit of pentacles. When you're done, thank the energies for being present in your life and move clockwise to the east. Clap or chant as you shift locations.

5. Once more, face east and honor the energies of the east once more. Again, thank the energies as you complete the full circle. Clap or chant as you shift locations.

6. Stand in the center of the area and look to the east and west. Use your hands to gather the energy from this line and place it the center. When you've honored and gathered the energy here, clap once and move to the next step.

7. Continue to stand in the center. Look to the north and south. Use your hands to gather the energy from this line and place it into the center. When you've honored and gathered the energy here, clap once and move to the next step.

8. Honor the energies of the above. Raise your arms high above your head and submit yourself to their inspection. For me these are the energies of the heavens; the unknown; and the realm of deity. When you're finished, thank them for being present in your life and drop your hands down to the center. Clap or chant as you shift locations.

9. Honor the energies of the below. Squat down to the ground or go as low as you can. Rest your hands (palms down) on the floor. Submit yourself to their inspection. Think about how the below supports you and connects you to a lineage of the past. It grounds you in your endeavors. When you're finished, thank them for being

present in your life and stand up. Clap, or chant, as you move to the next step.

10. Honor the energies of the center. Stand with your hands over your heart. Draw the four elements, the two lines, the above, and the below energies into this space. Honor the world you have built by standing in the present. You are now ready to perform your ritual.

When I am finished, I say some words indicating as such. I personally use the Diné phrase *yá'át'ééh*. Select words or phrases that resonate with you.

When you are finished, write down your experiences in your journal: How did this feel? Does it make the room feel different? If others are present, do they notice a different vibe in the space?

Tarot Throughout the Year

One of my favorite ways to ritualize tarot is to integrate the cards into various aspects of the year. Let the rituals in the following sections help you harness and access the energies of the cards to work in tune with the days, months, or years in your life.

I perform tarot rituals in spreads. They allow rituals for each holiday to shift and change, just like the passing of time. In fact, I'll provide you with a sample of the many ways I use the cards to honor the seasons and passing of time in this way.

You can also pick cards to meet your specific needs. For example, when I married my partner, I pulled the Two of Cups, the Empress, and the Lovers cards from my deck. These cards sat on the altar, next to our rings. The Two of Cups represented true and everlasting love. It sat up front and center during our ceremony. The Empress represented the goddess and held the creative energies that came together during our union. We kept the Lovers on our table to bless us with everlasting thirst for learning about each other and our relationship as it changes throughout the years.

Feel free to modify the rituals in this section to suit your needs. Replace my card suggestions with ones that work better for you, and look for cards containing energies better representing the seasons you're working with. Ready to see how this all works? Let's go!

Daily Spreads

Ritualize your daily draws. By now you've been pulling cards in the morning and recording tidbits about how the card showed up throughout your day. Add an element of ritual to the draws by lighting a candle, saying some words, or focusing on your day while shuffling the deck.

Re-evaluate your daily draw habit at this time. Does pulling a card in the morning work for you? Maybe you'd prefer to draw a card in the evening and do the reflection all at once. If you change your routine, be consistent about when you pull the card. Rituals work best when they are repeated over and over; if you train yourself to draw consistently, you will gain the power of connecting to the cards at the same time each day.

At the same time, don't make your draw rituals complex. You don't need to light incense and a candle, and call in all the elements or deities you know. Sometimes just sitting in the chair, drawing out your deck, and pulling a card is enough to put you in the mood.

For those of you who have been doing the daily draw (morning or evening) and want to try a more advanced spread, this three-card spread is for you.

Daily Forecast Spread

Sometimes, we want a little more information about our day than a single card can focus on. This three-card spread offers more information regarding your day. Use it to guide you through a specific event. Perhaps it can provide you with a game plan on how to get items on your list done and what people or situations to avoid.

The Daily Forcast Layout

Card One: What is going on? The first card represents an underlying theme of the day. Maybe it uncovers a lesson to learn, or the general attitude you might need to carry with you throughout your day.

Card Two: What should I avoid? This card represents emotions, situations, or hurdles you may face during the day. It's good to know what challenges may be in your way so you can adjust your attitude as they come up.

Card Three: What should my priorities be? This card represents what you should focus on for the day. It could be the first action item on your list, or it could let you know what you need in order to make space to ensure your tasks for the day get done.

Spreads to Honor the Lunar Cycle

From the specific focus of a single card draw we move onto the idea of using tarot to represent cycles in your life. We'll ease into using the cards as a way to recognize and honor these greater cycles by watching the monthly lunar phase.

Our current calendar system features thirteen lunar cycles a year, and the moon turns in four phases: new, waxing, full, and waning. Each of these phases has associations with various energies and attributes throughout traditions from various cultures and spiritual practices. The next four spreads honor each phase; use them during each lunar cycle to gain insight.

Pick one month and research when the new, waxing, full, and waning moon occurs. Mark these four dates down in your notebook. Put reminders of the dates and times in your calendar. When the date arrives, locate the corresponding spread and draw your cards. You can dress up the spreads by lighting candles, playing music, or even cleansing yourself with a warm shower before you pull the cards.

New Moon Phase

The new moon lunar energy happens when the moon appears as a slight sliver of light. Use the new moon to help you plan and design projects and what you want to bring into your life within the current month. The following ritual is good to use during the new moon to attune yourself to the new moon energies.

The New Moon Phase Layout

Card One: What should I work on this month?

Card Two: How can the energy of the new moon help me health-wise?

Card Three: How can the energy of the new moon help me generate new ideas?

Card Four: What will this new moon bring into my life?

Waxing Moon Phase

The period between the new and full phases is known as the Waxing Moon Phase. Look up at the sky and watch as the moon grows from a slim sliver of light to its full, round shape. When the moon is waxing, bring your cards out to create spreads that can help you attract the items, goals, and situations you desire to be present in your life.

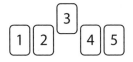

The Waxing Moon Phase Layout

Card One: What do I need to know about this waxing phase? This card shows energies around beginning new projects. It could show you what you bring into this situation.

Card Two: How will this project take shape? This card can show outside influences and other significant events shaping the birth of your desire.

Card Three: What should the project's intention be? This card shows what lesson, theme, or challenge you will learn from the project. This card carries the most weight.

Card Four: What does the project need to succeed? This card shows you what you need to do to make the project a success.

Card Five: What is my next step to take? This card helps determine what the next best step to take in the course of the project.

Full Moon Phase

When the moon is seen as a bright and shining disc up in the sky, it is full. The moon is full for about three days out of each month. The full moon is one of the most powerful times in the lunar phase, and has been notorious throughout all of human history for having strange effects on people. The full moon is said to inspire lunacy (the word itself is even created from the Latin word for moon, *luna*). During this powerful time, you have the full lunar powers at your fingertips.

Full moon energy is the perfect time to create spreads to manifest goals and dreams into your reality. It's also time to empower yourself and get you to where you want to be. Some witches put their decks or other magical tools under the light from the full moon to charge them.

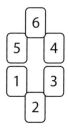

The Full Moon Phase Layout

Card One: What decision can you make to help express your potential? This card shows you areas or old patterns of thinking that may need to be let go or dropped.

Card Two: What action can you take on here to help you manifest your goals? This card gives you advice on the first small, action step you can take to make this dream a reality. Pay close attention to it.

Card Three: What can you do to fully express your gifts? This card may show blocks you may need to address.

Card Four: How can you protect your personal power so you aren't overwhelmed? Manifesting dreams requires you to focus on what you need. This card shows you how to keep your energy and time close to your heart so you can accomplish this goal in addition to living a full life.

Card Five: How can you best develop your intuition? The full moon affects intuitive gifts, so this card can help show you ways to extend your abilities. Court cards could suggest mentors or teachers.

Card Six: What blessings can the full moon bestow upon you at this time? This card shows gifts the full moon has for you.

Waning Moon Phase

The period when the moon fades from fullness and starts heading toward the darkness is known as the waning moon. When you look up at the night sky, you can see the moon change from a full round disc in the sky to a sliver of crescent light.

When the moon is in its waning phase, you can use these days to banish the people, situations, or habits you want out of your life. This includes emotions, situations, habits, ailments, or people no longer serving a positive influence in your life. Use the following spread to get you started on how to harness the power of the waning moon and bring its power into your life.

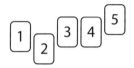

The Waning Moon Phase Layout

Card One: Where is my energy being drained? This card can shows you areas needing improvement.

Card Two: How can I slow down and allow this situation to unfold naturally? In this day and age, we move quickly. This card shows ways to slow down, rest, and stop forcing situations you are in to suit your needs.

Card Three: How can I accept what life has given me? Depression can hit during waning moon phases. This card helps you accept where you are in life. You are exactly where you need to be at this moment.

Card Four: What should I let go in order to grow? This card shows what you may have outgrown and can let go.

Card Five: Where is transformation occurring in my life?
This card shows you where the growth is in your life.
Expansion follows after the old has been removed.

Rituals for Each Season

Having visited how tarot rituals operate through a cycle of
the lunar month, let's push this motif one step further. Just as
there are four phases of the moon, our planet has four seasonal
phases. Again, there are many ways you can use the cards to
help you experience the energies of the seasons.

Many tarot decks themselves are structured to include the
elements of each season. Looking at even your basic deck, for
example, we see that each minor arcana suit has an associated
season that is shown in the cards. Of course, many readers
have their own variants and while I base mine off the Rider-
Waite-Smith system, I have my own personal tastes. You may
find that the decks you own and use have different styles of
seasons that differ, and that's fine. Use what you know and
stick with it.

In the following rituals, I use my associations for the spread
determinations. Feel free to replace them with your own and
set up your decorations as you desire.

EXERCISE: DETERMINING SEASONAL ASSOCIATIONS

How do you determine which suits correspond to which seasons? Easy—take out your deck and break it into five piles:
major arcana, wands, cups, swords, and pentacles.

Set aside the major arcana. Select one of the minor packs to work with. Lay down all the cards in the suit. Look at the images. Are there any weather cues? If you're using a non-traditional deck, sometimes I find that color palettes can tell seasonal stories.

For example:

When I set out all my minor arcana suits, the story I see is:

• Swords are equated to spring

• Wands are summer

• Cups are autumn

• Pentacles are winter

Once you have connection seasons to suits, you are now ready to test out the following seasonal rituals.

Spring Ritual

Ah, spring … the first season of our calendar year. Trees and flowers begin to replenish their limbs with buds, the animals grow new coats, and my allergies go nuts with all the pollen. In this season, we see the fruits of new ideas, the ability to seed new plants, and we're ready to head outside and enjoy warmer weather. The suit of swords is associated with spring. Look at the image of the three of swords, with the rain flowing down to wash away the negative and bring in the growth and new.

Spring is a time of renewal and the perfect time to begin a new tradition of seasonal tarot ritual. A few weeks before spring begins (in the northern hemisphere, these months are March through May), think about the colors and symbols you associate with this time.

My personal associations include:

- Colors: pastels, pink, light blue

- Animals: rabbits, lambs, llamas

- Flowers: daffodils, tulips, honeysuckle

- Scents: sage, strawberry

- Stones: clear quartz, rose quartz

These colors and items are used to decorate our altar table so when we work on our spring ritual we have reminders of the season surrounding us. Dress the table with your chosen color of spring, add a few fresh cut flowers to a vase, or place other trinkets (stones, statues, et cetera) around the space.

When you've finished decorating your altar table, use the following Spring Tarot ritual to draw inspiration. Separate the major arcana and the swords from your deck. Draw a major arcana card from the top of your deck. On the first day of each spring month, pull a card from the swords pack. Record your thoughts and meanings for each card in your journal.

During the last week of the last month, I'll look at the cards, write about what message each one brought me. I then put the cards back into the deck and begin creating summer's altar design.

The Spring Ritual Layout

Card One: The topic of the season.

Card Two: What insight does the first spring month bring me?

Card Three: What insight does the second month bring me?

Card Four: What insight does the last month bring me?

Summer Ritual

Summer months remind me of family vacations, going to summer camps (and now that I am an adult, festivals), being active outside, and reading books. I associate this season with hot weather, swimming, and wearing my fun fae clothing. Summertime is a period of living life at its fullest. We're able to run around outside for long hours, and all the trees and flowers are in full bloom. The local wildlife comes out and is more visible. I associate wands with summer. Most of the images are outside and in warm settings. The Queen of Wands card features sunflowers, whose gigantic flowers bloom in the summer.

Summer is a time of activity and warmth. It's our second stop on our seasonal tarot ritual. Summer months are June through August. As spring winds down, you'll remove the altar dressings and spring cards and redecorate your table in the colors and symbols of summer:

- Colors: gold, deep green, dark blue

- Animals: butterflies, dogs, hummingbirds

- Flowers: sunflowers, snapdragons, lavender

- Scents: lavender, pine, honeysuckle

- Stones: tiger's eye, amazonite, aquamarine

These colors and items are used to decorate our altar table so when we work on our summer ritual, we have reminders of the season surrounding us. Dress the table with your chosen color of summer. Add summer flowers to your vase, set candles on the table, and place other trinkets (stones, statues, et cetera) around the space.

When you finish decorating your altar table, use the following Summer Tarot ritual to draw inspiration. Separate the major arcana and the wands from your deck. Draw a major arcana card from the top of your deck. On the first day of each summer month, pull a card from the wands pack. Record your thoughts and meanings for each card in your journal.

During the last week of the last month, I'll look at the cards and write about the message each one brought me. I then put the cards back into the deck and begin creating autumn's altar design.

The Summer Ritual Layout

Card One: The topic of the season

Card Two: What insight does the first summer month bring me?

Card Three: What insight does the second month bring me?

Card Four: What insight does the last month bring me?

Autumn Ritual

Autumn months remind me of foggy mornings; red, gold, and orange leaves; curling up on the sofa with a good book and a mug of chai; sleeping in; and Halloween. I associate this season with rain (in the Pacific Northwest it's constantly raining during autumn), wearing multiple layers of clothing, and breaking out the warm flannel blankets. Autumn days grow short and we get in touch with our inner landscapes, clearing the clutter for the next year.

The suit of cups is associated with autumn because many of the scenes feature yellow backgrounds that remind me of the changing colors of the leaves or the sunset. On the Three of Cups, we see a scene of people dancing around an abundant garden of fruits and vegetables that ripen and then are ready for harvest.

Summer winds down, and we then prep for autumn and the coming winter. The months of September, October, and November are our third stop on our seasonal tarot ritual tour. As summer comes to a close, you'll remove the altar dressings and summer cards and decorate your table in the colors and symbols of autumn:

- Colors: red, brown, yellow

- Animals: hawks, squirrels

- Flowers: pumpkins, marigolds, carnations

- Scents: chai, pumpkin pie, patchouli

- Stones: agate, lapis lazuli

These colors and items are used to decorate our altar table so when we work on our autumn ritual we have reminders of the season surrounding us. Dress the table with your chosen color of autumn. Add a few fresh cut flowers to a vase. Place other trinkets (stones, statues, et cetera) around the space.

When you finish decorating your altar table, use the following Autumn Tarot ritual to draw inspiration. Separate the major arcana and the cups from your deck. Draw a major arcana card from the top of your deck. On the first day of each autumn month, pull a card from the cups pack. Record your thoughts and meanings for each card in your journal.

During the last week of the last month, I'll look at the cards and write about the message each one brought me. I then put the cards back into the deck and begin creating winter's altar design.

The Autumn Ritual Layout

Card One: The topic of the season

Card Two: What insight does the first month of autumn bring me?

Card Three: What insight does the second month bring me?

Card Four: What insight does the last month bring me?

Winter Ritual

Winter is the coldest season. Snow, going sledding and snow-shoeing, the cheer of the winter holiday season, and bundling in warm hoodies reminds me of this season. Winter is about resting and being close to friends and family and sharing yummy foods to tide us over until the first plants peek through the cold soil of spring. Here in the Pacific Northwest, we get a lot of rain in the winter, so I associate this season with rain, the disappearance of the sun from the sky, and sharing good stories with my friends during the long evenings. I associate the pentacles with winter since the cards depict a lot of cold scenes and barren areas. Just look at the Five of Pentacles—two people walk in a visibly cold winter scene.

Winter has us going deep within ourselves (and staying inside), to stay warm and safe until spring picks up again. As our last stop on season ritual tour, it happens during December, January, and February. As autumn winds down, you'll remove the altar dressings and autumn cards and decorate your table in the colors and symbols of winter:

- Colors: white, black, green

- Animals: bears, arctic foxes, wolves

- Flowers: holly, poinsettias, mistletoe

- Scents: hot chocolate, yule logs

- Stones: moonstone, obsidian

These colors and items are used to decorate our altar table so when we work on our winter ritual, we have reminders of the season surrounding us. Dress the table with your chosen color of winter. Use a lot of candles to brighten the space up. Add a few twigs and maybe place a bowl with water or snow on the table. Place other trinkets (stones, statues, et cetera) around the space.

When you finish decorating your altar table, use the following Winter Tarot ritual to draw inspiration. Separate the major arcana and the pentacles from your deck. Draw a major arcana card from the top of your deck. On the first day of each winter month, pull a card from the pentacles pack. Record your thoughts and meanings for each card in your journal.

During the last week of the last month, I'll look at the cards and write about the message each one brought me. I then put the cards back into the deck and begin creating spring's altar design.

The Winter Ritual Layout

Card One: The topic of the season

Card Two: What insight does the first month of winter bring me?

Card Three: What insight does the second month bring me?

Card Four: What insight will the last month bring me?

The Year-Long Elemental Working

This final exercise utilizes all the tips and tricks you've learned up to this point. In this ritual cycle, you'll be pulling cards monthly and acting out their recommendations. It's a unique journey that can help you examine who you are now and inspire you to manifest the person you want to become.

January first is an important date in our culture. On this date, we set new goals and make all sorts of promises to ourselves—to lose weight; save money; or do more. Soon after, we lose sight of these lofty achievements and go back to old habits and patterns. The power of using a yearlong ritual and incorporating a tarot element into it can help you achieve those goals by keeping you motivated and focused.

This practice was inspired by Taylor Ellwood, who outlined a similar process in his book *Inner Alchemy*. We refer to this working as a year-long elemental practice, and I have been doing it for many years now, as it's a wonderful way to examine one aspect of life and push it to a new height. Yes, there have been failures, but I've learned from those experiences. In fact, I started incorporating tarot into my structure so I could see more and achieve greater results. Tarot has become a great tool to measure the changes I create within my life.

You'll need to set aside space on your altar for at least twelve cards. These cards will be displayed for an entire year. Each card you lay out is a part of the story of your journey into learning the element and integrating it into yourself.

The Year-Long Elemental working has several steps; the rest of this chapter walks you through each part.

Preparation

Entering a year-long study is a worthy, exciting, and challenging endeavor. And in order to be successful, a bit of preparatory work is required.

First you need to brainstorm a list of elements you want to work with. This can be as simple as going with one of the five traditional elements (earth, air, fire, water, spirit) or you can use your creativity and create your own element. I loosely define an element as any aspect, adjective, or personal trait you want to integrate into your core being. The first year I did this working, I chose to work with the element of movement because I wanted to work on having a dedicated exercise regimen.

I keep a running list of elements in one of my books of magical stuff. When it gets close to the next year, I look over the list and select one. You can also add new elements to this list whenever one pops up for you. They can have particular meanings to you or you can choose to develop a personal meaning throughout the year. Some of the other elements from my list are: silence, hearing, creativity, writing, exploration.

Once you have a list of suitable elements, you'll need a few other items before you begin your year long journey:

Your chosen element. Decide which element you'll use from the brainstorm list. You can draw the element at random or use a pendulum. This is the one element you'll dedicate yourself to working with over the next year. During the time this manuscript was drafted, I was four months into a personal working with the element of alchemy. Since this element was most apparent in my life, I will use it as the main example throughout this section.

The change or desired outcome you want this element to help you achieve. This statement of change is probably also the most important aspect of the yearlong working. This statement helps set the measurement of change you want to reach for when the work is finished. It will also remind you why you are doing this process when you forget. What do you want to achieve in working with this element? Why is this working important now? These are good questions to keep in mind as you prep for this adventure. In my alchemy working, I wrote:

> Alchemy is the culmination of looking at the core parts of myself and synthesizing something new out of it. I want to push the boundaries of my tarot knowledge and see what I can do to create a better brand for how I help others with the cards. I chose this element based from several discussions with my friends about what I wanted to do with my tarot life and business. Years ago I spent a lot of time focusing on tarot and traveling and teaching. I attended the Reader's Studio for the first time, and when I got home from this event, I received a lot of clarity in that I needed to make the cards a central figure in both my working life and spiritual life. Everything I wanted to do in my life moving forward goes hand in hand with tarot.

Therefore, with this in mind, I defined my intent for my year-long alchemical working: Transformation of myself and synthesis of all the knowledge I have learned throughout the years of studying and playing with tarot.

I also had a clear picture in my head of what I wanted the next year to look like: a published tarot author, improving my reading style to help give my clients a clear roadmap in attaining their dreams, and growing my tarot business in the areas of gaining clients and teaching.

With all this in mind, the part of alchemy where the practitioners practiced turning lead into gold seemed to fit rather well in my notions of pushing myself beyond my limits to become something new.

The deity exemplar you want to work with. This is just a fancy term for someone or some being you interview and then ask to use as a companion while you're on this ride. Your deity exemplar can be a god(dess) from a real and known pantheon, a person you know or admire, an animal totem or spirit guide, or a fictional character.

There are many ways of finding your deity. You can use sources from your favorite movies or television shows, religions, pantheons, or even other versions of yourself. The first step in picking your deity is to list names of people you think may fit into the element you've chosen. Then go through the list and interview each person: load up a mental version of the person in your head and the ask them questions (just like a real interview) about how they can help you best learn the element. Find out what they can teach you, and what their limits are.

I like to take walks and interview the candidates at that time. This way, I get some good exercise and have a better idea of which deity will help teach me the element so I can reach my goal.

When you have talked to all your deities, contemplate the best choice for who you want to work with for a year. After you have picked your deity, talk to them once more and ask them to give you a symbol you can use to invoke their energies when you need it.

Research on element and deity. Spend a month or more to research your deity before you start your first ritual. Once you have selected the best candidate, continue to research all the information you can find on them. The more complete image of the deity you have, the better the experience becomes because you will have so many details to make the deity come alive visually and in sound.

When I first started thinking about using alchemy as my elemental focus for this year, I had a small list of names of those I wanted to work with. In the beginning, I didn't know about real-world alchemy, the history, its processes, or the outcomes, so I had to do some research. I knew that someone named Nicolas Flamel had something to do with it. In looking at the Wikipedia page on alchemy, I also discovered it was associated with the Egyptian god Thoth. So right off the bat I had two potentials … but I wanted to try something different.

One of my favorite fiction series is *Mistborn*, by Brandon Sanderson. In the books, characters use a creative magical system wherein they imbibe metals into their bodies, and different metals like tin, pewter, and aluminum affect the world in different ways. This magic system fascinated me, and I saw it as a source of how to use alchemy on a metaphysical level. It also seemed to fit well with my intent to recreate myself. So I tossed two characters from the first book in the series, Kelsier and Vin, into the hat.

With my list complete, I started my interview process. I asked each potential deity questions to see what they had to say about my ideas and whether or not they felt comfortable in teaching me the principles of alchemy so that I could achieve the desired transformations. The only one who wholeheartedly wanted to work with me was Kelsier, so I had my deity and was ready to move on.

Despite having read the *Mistborn* series with its world still fresh in my mind, I knew I had to do some more research. I needed a reminder about the metals used in the series, what they did, and how the process worked. This was an important aspect to this project because in order to transform myself, I had to know what base metals I was working with. You can't mix two elements together before you have a thorough understanding of what outcome tossing them together would have. I returned to the internet to get more background research. I also had to figure out how to apply the magic system of the *Mistborn* books into the year-long tarot workings I'd be doing—I wasn't going to imbibe real metals and expect fantastical outcomes.

In addition to relearning about the *Mistborn* metals, I also needed more information on exactly what alchemy is. Since

I'm no alchemist, I thought it important to have a background idea of what this process was and where it came from. To that end, I gathered a list of books and read them. I also found two symbols to work with Kelsier: one was a hand motion used to summon him when I had questions, and the other I used as a meditation focus to help me set my transformational intent.

A virtual meeting space. A virtual meeting space is a room you set up in your mind. It contains items and space for you and the deity during your sessions. For me, this mental room is where I talk to my deity and go to do any exercises they teach. While I have physical ritual spaces in my home, I knew I'd be doing most of the work in the room I created in my mind. Therefore, using the power of my imagination I created a safe environment where Kelsier and I could work together to manipulate the various metals together safely. Another benefit of having a virtual space is that you can modify it as the teaching process unfolds.

As far as my physical space was concerned, I set up a wooden card holder for the twelve cards I would be setting up during the year. Test out your tables and spaces to make sure they can hold all the cards you'll be setting out. Keeping the cards out helps when you want to see your progress and ask detailed questions of your deity.

Got your element, statement, deity, virtual meeting space, and altar space prepped? Then you are ready to perform your Dedication ritual.

Dedication Ritual

The Dedication ritual is your first step in reaching your desired outcome. In this ritual you dedicate yourself to the element, formally enter a mentorship with your deity, and promise to schedule meetings every month to work with them to achieve your goals. The ritual outline is flexible enough, so that it can work in your existing schedule. You can also perform other workings you want your deity to oversee at this time.

You can pick any day to perform your dedication ritual; I prefer using the first day of my birth month. Other good months include the first of a new year, a new lunar cycle, or any other auspicious dates you may have.

Set aside about an hour to perform this ritual on the day you chose. Let everyone know that you need to be alone. Turn off the alarms, mute your phone, and rid yourself of any other distractions. Performing your dedications as the activity in the morning works well while your mind is fresh.

Dedication Ritual Script

Gather the following tools when you are ready to start the ritual:

- Your ritual tarot deck (if you only have one deck, I suggest you get a second)

- Any candles, incense, or other focus-improving implements

- Your journal and a pen

- A piece of paper with your deity's
  name or image on it

- A piece of paper with your element's symbol on it

Go to your altar and set the space up for your working. Take some time to ground and focus on the task at hand. Light candles, incense, or do activities to help you focus. If you put any incense or candles on the altar, go ahead and light them now. When you are ready, follow this script.

> *Today I dedicate myself to the element of* (element name). *I call upon my mentor,* (deity's name), *who will guide me through the next twelve months of learning about my element and how I can effectively use it in my life.*

Place the image of your deity on the altar. Place the element's symbol on the altar and focus on it. Allow it to help you invoke the deity. Close your eyes and stand in your virtual space. Wait patiently until your deity appears in the space with you. Give them time to inspect the space and give their approval. It's not uncommon for some deities to modify or request additions. When you are done making adjustments, continue with the script.

> Say: *Welcome,* (name of deity). *I call you here today because I want you to help teach me the ways of* (element name). *Please guide me through the process of working with this element that will bring me clarity and insight into my life during the next twelve months. I promise to listen to you and do any internal work necessary to improve my life.*

Close your eyes and meditate with the deity. Your deity may offer words of wisdom or set some ground rules down first. Sometimes they may want you to do more prep work before you start your first month's lesson, sometimes they will just wait and watch you. If your deity requires you to do some homework, write it down in your journal and make a conscious effort to work on it. When you both are done talking, continue on with the script.

Take out your deck. Shuffle the cards while thinking about the following question: "What aspect of (element name) should I focus on this month?"

Pull a card from the deck.

Spend some time looking at this card. What does the card mean to you and how does it relate to the element working? If you aren't sure what the message is, you can pull more cards for clarification. Once you understand the message, return the clarification cards back to the deck. Write down any responses or insights into your journal.

When you are done, thank the deity and the elements for bearing witness by putting out the candles or incense. You can leave the deity image and the element symbol on the altar for the next year.

Journal about your experiences and thoughts from this ritual. If you were assigned any homework, begin working on that as soon as you can.

Alchemical Dedication Ritual Example

June first started out like any other ordinary day: first day of a new month, new moon, and a solar eclipse. I couldn't have asked for a more auspicious energetic setting to send me off on a new magical journey. I woke up and immediately went into my ritual room, excited to hold this dedication ritual.

I lit a yellow candle for air, the color I associate with new beginnings, intelligence, and brainstorming. I then lit a dragon's blood incense stick, as dragon's blood is good for new beginnings and powerful magical workings. (This scent is also quite potent, so use it lightly.) Using the incense stick, I lit a red candle for fire, and a blue one for water. I don't light candles for earth; instead, I use that time to ground myself and open a connection to the planet beneath my feet.

Feeling grounded and stable, I recited the above script, dedicating myself to alchemy and Kelsier. I spent some time talking to him in the space I created for him. I was looking for his approval as well as for any words he wanted to tell me. His first request of me was to "know my metals." I took this to mean that before I could work to combine any two metals together, or in his terms, "burn" a metal effectively, it was essential to be familiar with each individual item and its effects. Therefore, I knew that one of my first homework assignments was to study my metals—in this case, perform a 78-day tarot card study. In the study, I was to imbibe each card's essence and craft my own LWB of meanings for each one. At the end, the hope would be that I'd end up with a good base foundation for which to burn and combine my metals.

At this point, I deviated from the script a bit because I had two extra side workings to perform: a new moon/eclipse ritual reading, and also a ritual to cleanse and initiate four new tarot decks into my service. The first deck was the new Gaian Tarot, to be used in my magical workings. I wanted Kelsier to watch over this process since this deck would be used in conjunction with his teachings.

After these side tasks were performed, I refocused my attention to the dedication script. I pulled a single card from the deck to help me understand what to focus my alchemical learnings on for the next month. I drew Awakening (otherwise known as Judgment) from the Gaian Tarot. It took me some time to crack the meaning of this card; I thought about all the definitions of this card. I read the card-specific information from Joanna Powell Colbert's companion book and immediately felt the gears click into place; it was such an auspicious card for the first month. I translated the message as thus: I am awakening from an old perspective, an old way of going about my business and performing magics to working on the wonder that is transformational alchemy and the serious study of tarot and the power of integrating all this into my life as a whole.

I placed the Awakening card on my altar so I would see and visit it daily. It would become the focus on my meditations—the concepts of awakening and "knowing my metals" for the next thirty days.

I closed my ritual and then wrote notes about the experience in my book of shadows.

After the Dedication ritual has ended, you are under the tutelage of your deity. Spend time during this first month in meditation. Talk to your deity and let them help you understand the path you are taking. Do the homework that you are assigned, and when you need it, invoke your deity with any questions you have. Feel free to sit down and do any other spell castings or rituals that may be required during this month.

Use the next ritual, the Monthly Check-in, for the next eleven months on the first of every month to learn what the next steps are and gain more information.

Monthly Check-In Ritual

The Dedication ritual marked the first month of your year-long journey. At the beginning of each month for the next eleven months, you will go back to your altar and perform this Monthly Check-in ritual. Use the time in this space to talk to your deity about your homework, road blocks, or any other questions that come to mind. You can also spend more time speaking to your deity if you want.

Don't worry if you feel like you have no idea what you are doing or you are unsure how each month fits in together. Sometimes it won't become clear to you until you have moved on and are working on a new element. Trust yourself, the deity, your connection to spirit, and that the process has your best interests at heart. The working is doing what it needs to do to get you to your goals.

When you are done, you should have a total of twelve cards on your altar table and twelve, or more, journal entries in your journal.

Monthly Check-In Ritual Script

Gather the following tools when you are ready to start the ritual:

- Your ritual deck

- Any candles, incense, or other focus-improving implements

- Your journal and a pen

Go to your altar and set the space up for your working. Take some time to ground and focus on the task at hand. Light candles and incense, or do other activities to get yourself into that headspace. If you've put any incense or candles on the altar, go ahead and light them now. When you are ready, follow this script. Invoke your deity to watch over this process.

Take out your deck and shuffle the cards while focusing on the question, "What aspect of (element name) should I focus on this month?"

Pull a card from the deck.

Spend some time looking at this card—what does it mean to you and how does it relate to the element working? If you aren't sure what the message is, you can pull more cards for clarification. Once you understand the message, return the clarification cards to the deck. Write down any responses or insights into your journal.

When you are done, turn to your deity and discuss the month's focus. See if your deity has any insights to offer and any more homework for you to do.

When you are done, thank the deity and the elements for bearing witness by putting out the candles or incense.

Journal your experiences and thoughts from this ritual. If you were assigned any homework, begin working on it as soon as you can.

Alchemical Working Example

July first found me in my ritual room once again. As before, I lit the yellow candle and sat in front of my altar with my Gaian Tarot deck in hand. I closed my eyes and shuffled the cards while reflecting on what I learned during my first month of alchemy. I thought about the books I read, the processes I learned, and the LWB I was making. When I felt a slight tug on my hands to stop shuffling, I pulled out the next card: Temperance. I laughed and smiled—in tarot, the Temperance card is also known as alchemy. I figured that in this month, I was supposed to start combining the elements to learn how they worked together to create a third element.

I then called upon Kelsier and told him what I was thinking. He seemed to be happy and reminded me that I could do some simple elemental experiments in our space by combining the five elements we had set up in circle together. I thanked him for his wisdom and went about my business.

The Closing Ritual

The Closing ritual happens at the end of the last month of your Year-long Elemental ritual. I do it one week before the last day of the month. This closing ritual has two purposes. It gives you any last-minute chances to talk to your deity and receive any wisdom, or find out how you two can chat outside of the working if you need their advice. It also allows you to gently close the working so you can prepare on the next elemental working, if you plan on doing everything again.

You may find some overlap in this month where you are preparing the next year's element and doing current elemental working, which is quite natural—just remember that you are still focused on the current element and cannot start working on the next one yet. You are still dedicated to the current element and are required to do the homework and work on the items they have laid out for you. Who knows, perhaps your current deity can give you insight into what element to tackle next? Don't worry about losing the connection you have with your deities, they'll be there when you need them. All you have to do use their symbol.

Closing Ritual Outline and Script

Gather the following tools when you are ready to start the ritual:

- Your ritual deck

- Any candles, incense, or other focus-improving implements

- Your journal and a pen

Go to your altar and set the space up for your working. Take some time to ground and focus on the task at hand. Light candles and incense, or do activities to help you focus. If you put any incense or candles on the altar, go ahead and light them now. When you are ready, follow this script.

Look at the array of cards on your table. Think about how you were at the beginning of this journey. Think about how each card on your altar helped influence you every month during your journey. Write about the experience you have been through and all that you have learned along the way. I like to take all twelve cards and write the story of the year from the beginning to the final month. This exercise helps solidify each month's lesson and experiences and ties it all back into the year's element.

Take out your deck and shuffle the cards while focusing on the question, "What overall lesson should I take away from having this experience with (element name here)?"

Pull a card from the deck.

Spend some time looking at this card. What does the card mean to you and how does it relate to the element working? If you aren't sure what the message is, you can pull more cards for clarification. Once you understand the message, return the clarification cards back to the deck. Write down any responses or insights into your journal.

When you have completed journaling about the card, invoke your deity and tell them what you have learned. See if your deity has any more work for you to do or insight to offer. If necessary, make arrangements to see them outside of this working if you desire to continue the connection you have built. Thank your deity for their time and help along the path, and offer any libations to them in their name and honor.

Now remove all twelve tarot cards from the altar. I usually start at the twelfth card and pick it up and work my way backward until the first card is back in my hands. I then set these cards on top of the original deck, shuffle the cards for a bit, and then tap the cards three times with one hand. This resets the deck and gets it ready for the next working.

When you are done, thank the deity and the elements for bearing witness by putting out the candles or incense.

Journal about your experiences and thoughts about this ritual. If you plan to move on with the next element, you should continue or start your preparation work now.

Alchemy Working Example

In the last week of May, I went back into my ritual room. I lit three candles on my altar (yellow, red, and blue; one for each element) and grounded to complete the cycle of bringing in the elements. I then called out to Kelsier, my deity, and invited him into our alchemical space. I thanked him for all his help and advice. He smiled and nodded and told me that I did some good, deep work on myself. I asked him if he'd be willing to appear to me whenever I needed, and he agreed.

I then brought out my deck and pulled a single card to wrap up my alchemy working. The card was the Chariot, which had the message that the work is ongoing and the path to build my tarot empire was long but would be worth it in the end.

I thanked Kelsier once more as I closed the ritual and thought about the next element I'd be working on.

For further study and reflection on the topics included in this chapter, look for the following books:

Amaral, Geraldine, and Nancy Brady Cunningham. *Tarot Celebrations: Honoring the Inner Voice.* York Beach, ME: Weiser, 1997.

Ellwood, Taylor. *Inner Alchemy: Energy Work and the Magic of the Body.* Stafford, UK: Immanion Press, 2006.

Kraig, Donald Michael. *Tarot & Magic.* St. Paul, MN: Llewellyn Publications, 2002.

Jette, Christine. *Tarot for All Seasons: Celebrating the Days & Nights of Power.* St. Paul, MN: Llewellyn Publications, 2001.

Morrison, Dorothy. *Everyday Tarot Magic: Meditation & Spells.* St. Paul, MN: Llewellyn Publications, 2002.

Part 3
Putting It
All Together

Chapter 9

Taking Tarot to the Next Level

Connecting to Others

By the end of this chapter you'll:

- Learn to read for others

- Discover a thriving global tarot community

- Locate events to attend

By now, you've spent a lot of time learning about tarot. You've learned how to make sense of the cards—you've identified their symbols, investigated their colors, and learned what messages they have for you. You've personalized their meanings and recorded them in your own Tarot PDA. You've learned how to make spreads and divine answers from them. You've done some meditations, invocations, and card rituals. You are now on your way to creating a tarot-inspired life.

In this final chapter, we'll look at some of the ways you can take tarot to the next level. If you haven't tried reading for others, I'll guide you through the process of what a typical reading looks like for me. I'll also share with you some tips on connecting to others online; and I'll give you a brief idea of what fun tarot conferences can be.

Reading for Others

At some point in every reader's career comes a time when they want to break free from the learning track and experience the world of reading for others. You will know this feeling as wanting to "go pro" or just having an intense desire to help others through the power of tarot; it happened to me many years ago. If you haven't started reading the cards for others, then you're in for a real treat.

Tarot draws people in. It doesn't matter whether or not the client believes the cards are good or bad … when a pack of cards appears, people turn their heads to see what's going on. It happens to me wherever I go. Inevitably, looks lead to curious people wondering if I can "read the cards for them," or they say "do me next" as if it's a parlor game that has no potential bearing on their lives. I'll draw a card or two with them sometimes if I'm not on a schedule; I like giving people a small a taste of what tarot does. More often than not, however, I don't—it takes time to do a proper reading for someone. Readings can also have profound effects on your client's life.

If you've never done a reading for others, it can be overwhelming and a bit scary. You want to give them your best, and you also want to honor your own integrity. That's where this section comes in. I've taken the time to break down the process of reading cards for others. You can use the information here as an outline for your own readings or a starting point for crafting your own practice.

Reading Formats

There is no right or wrong way to do readings for others. I've done many readings over the years and have identified three core parts to a reading. which helps make the reading process easy. While this format is what I know and what works for me, I don't expect it to work for everyone. The only thing that makes a reader is practice. Play around with layouts, formats, reading lengths, and so on to build up your experience and style. It's taken me more than fifteen years to develop a system which works best for both my style and what I want to offer my clients.

The three key parts to a reading are the introduction phase, the reading phase, and the wrap-up phase. Each stage serves a purpose and can take as long as it needs to accomplish its goals. The ultimate point of a reading is to make sure your client's question or topic has been satisfactorily answered.

If you operate on timed readings (half- or hour-long sessions) you'll want to time the readings you give to make sure you're able to discuss all the points your client wants out of the reading into the allotted time. Clients rarely seem to want to pay for the extra time, although they *do* seem to want that extra information!

Introduction Phase

Make your client feel comfortable the moment they sit down. Shake their hand and tell them your name. Be genuinely pleased to see them. Smile and focus all your attention to their needs and desires. Lean forward and pay attention to what they have to say. I break the ice by asking them if they've ever had a reading before. If they haven't, I let them know they're in for a real treat. Sometimes I'll let them play with my cards to demystify them.

Once the client relaxes, ask them what brought them to you today. People will come to you with a story: they face challenges in their life and hope you can help them sort out what is going on. They seek answers, so take time to listen to them. Your job here is to figure out the heart of their story—what is it they want to get from the cards? Help guide them into forming a question they can ask the cards.

Sometimes a client will sit down in front of you with no idea what to ask; they are simply curious to see how the process works. When this happens, give them some time to tell you what is happening in their life. Alternatively, you can offer some generic questions for them to choose from. If there is any time left in their reading, you can use it to expand on what the cards said or pull more cards from the questions that came up during the primary discussion. Usually I'll ask them what challenges they're facing in life that could use some perspective and jump into the reading from there.

The last objective of this phase is to set reading expectations. Let your client know how deep you can go in examining their reading with the time and payment. If time doesn't matter to your practice and the question is a deeply rooted one, let them know that your reading may take a few sessions to unravel. You can schedule more appointments if you believe their question will take more time than you have energy to give at that moment. If your client agrees, you can move to the next phase.

Two versions of the introduction phase happen in my practice. The first takes place when the client contacts me directly for a reading. In this situation I'll send the client an email with questions they need to answer before we lay down any cards. This accomplishes two objectives: it gives them the time and space they need to figure out what is going on and how they want to spend our time together, and it also lets them know I take reading tarot for others seriously. I want my clients to get the most out of the time we have together. Since my professional readings are time-based (hour-long sessions) I know I want to get right into helping my client the moment they sit down next to me.

The questions I ask as part of the introduction phase are:

1. Why do you seek consultation?

2. What concrete changes do you want to manifest in your life?

3. What are your objectives for our time together?

When I am at events, I often do not have the luxury of having clients know exactly what they're buying with their time. In this case, I shorten this process to quickly isolate a topic or question. Sometimes at events I'll create a "reading of the day" beforehand and use the same spread over and over as a way to get new clients interested in how my reading style can assist them. If they have a specific question that cannot be answered in the time allotted, I ask them to set up a new appointment at a later time and date.

Once we've had time to know one another and figure out the core of why they came to see me, the client and I go into the next phase of our reading, the actual reading itself.

Reading Phase

This is where the magic happens, where you take your deck out, suggest a spread, lay down some cards, and begin interpreting them for your client. It can be scary to read for others.

Your client came to you … out of all those other readers. They look to you to be their guide. They expect you to know things about the cards and give them what they need to know. You are expected to give them a good reading and an acceptable answer to their question. No pressure, right?

It's at this point in a reading where new readers develop blocks or forget the meanings of their cards. Before you begin, take a deep breath and relax. The cards know what is going on. All you need to do is look at the cards and decipher their messages. To get me started on reading and interpreting the cards for others, I do some or all of the following:

1. Relate cards to their position in the spread as it relates to their reading. If you are using a spread that has defined positions, the first step you can do is to figure out what the card in each position means. For example, if the position in a spread is "next step" and the card in that position is the Hierophant, tell your client they might want to talk to a spiritual counselor; if their question relates to education, maybe they should seek a mentor or teacher.

2. Look for patterns. What suits are represented? What suits are missing? When I see a a lack of cards from any particular suit or suits, I consider it to be a non-focus of the spread. For example, a lack of cup cards might suggest the client is

emotionally stable or isn't worried about the emotions of the situation. No pentacles? Sounds like the client is financially stable or happy.

3. What numbers are on the cards? The numbers give me an idea of where the client is in their journey or path relating to their question. If all the numbers are low, they may be just starting out. Similarly, look at the elements in the spread. What does it mean when your client gets three fiery wands cards?

4. If you use a free-form reading with no positions, look for the story of what the cards are saying. I'll move cards around and see what meanings and messages fall out from all the cards as they appear face up or are turned over. I'm not afraid to move cards around and see how it changes perspectives for my client. I've also been known to flip a card or two over if the image has a disturbing effect on my client.

If you draw a blank on a card and what it may mean, that's okay. It happens to everyone. When it happens to me, I'll sometimes name the card out loud which can often times trigger messages to say to the client. If that doesn't work, then I may ask the client to look at the card and tell me what they are seeing. If neither of you have any insight, it's okay to let them know this. Move on to another card. Alternatively, you can draw a new card to help clarify the previous one or replace the blank altogether.

As I move through each card in a reading, I like to weave a story. When a client comes to me for a reading, we may spend a few minutes on the first card but spend most of our time on the second card and then only a few minutes more on the last card. Every time a new card gets flipped over, I wrap up what we just talked about.

For example, in a reading I may say, "Well, you came to me wondering about how to get a new lover, so we pulled the Five of Wands. This card is a card of confusion and chaos. So perhaps you should lighten your work load. Then we pulled the Lovers card, and it suggested that you shouldn't focus so much on finding a soul mate but instead play the field and have some fun with potential suitors." By the time a client's reading is over, they are able to follow the story of the reading from one card to the next, they know how each card relates to another, and (hopefully) they retained the key points in their reading. It is this summary of the cards and the client's story that triggers the final phase of the reading.

Wrap-Up Phase

The wrap-up phase is the final step of a client reading. It comes after you have performed a reading for your client and are winding the reading down to a close. Three objectives happen in this phase. First, give the client time to reflect on what was discussed in their reading. You'll want to make sure they understand the information you spoke about. Give them time to ask questions. Summarize key points from the reading, answer any other questions they may have, and offer advice for what comes next.

If the reading included any good "homework" ideas or a next step for the client to take, make sure they follow through with doing the work so that their desired reading outcome will manifest. This may include getting their contact information for a follow-up call or asking them back for a second reading.

The wrap-up phase gives you time to accept the agreed upon payment, and make further reading appointments. This isn't the easiest to do, as clients usually want to give your reading time to sink in. In that case, I politely ask the client if they'd be willing to let me call them after a certain amount of time passes to remind them of their next reading.

There is one more action I do after the client has moved away from my table. I ground out and release any residual energy the person and the reading may have. This allows me to reset the stage and get ready for my next appointment or reading. This step becomes *especially* important when you are reading at psychic fairs or other events where you have a long line of new clients waiting to have their questions answered.

A Sample Reading

I created this sample reading to illustrate how the three stages of a reading work in a realistic way.

I am reading cards at a festival and am approached by a woman. She introduces herself as Becca, and I welcome her to sit at my table. She does, and we talk about what is going on in her life. Becca has never had a reading before, and she's not feeling too great about life. She says that she only has half an hour or less to spare but wants to try this out. She tells me that she recently lost her home in a tornado and wants to know what will happen next. I invite her to talk more about this event and how it feels. As Becca talks to me, she tells me that she's waiting on a settlement from the insurance company to help cover costs of a new apartment. I nod and realize that this is the heart of the matter. I ask Becca, "So if I hear you correctly, you want to know when you'll get the settlement and if this new apartment is right for you?"

With the topic set, I think about what layout to use. I decide that we will only draw two cards (this is a short session, after all), and I want to make sure we are able to go as deep as we can with these two questions. Becca agrees. I decide that the first card will represent what she can do to make sure she gets a settlement in a timely manner, and the second card will give her advice around this new apartment and what she can do to make it her home. Before we proceed, I ask Becca if this is acceptable. She smiles and tells me she likes the direction this is going.

I begin shuffling my deck while focusing my energy on Becca and how the universe can guide her into providing her the best life she can have. When I am ready, I put the deck face down on the table and tell Becca to cut the deck into two piles. I then tell her to pick which one represents the insurance claim and which one represents the new apartment option. She determines which piles go to which question, and I rub my hands together, eager to get her reading started.

I turn over the top card of the insurance settlement pile and preview the card. She's received the Ten of Swords. Instead of going into standard book knowledge about this card, I give Becca the chance to speak about what she sees and feels. I note her body language: she does not like the image of a person with the ten swords going through the body.

"I don't I like this," she begins. I look at her and try and embody what she is feeling. Looking down at the card with curiosity, I ask, "Why do you say that? What is going on?" She frowns again and says, "Well this guy is lying in a puddle of his own blood, and I am not so sure I like that. It appears as if he has been stabbed and killed with all those swords coming out of his back."

We continue following Becca's train of thought. If this situation is bad, it could represent her fears about not getting the settlement at all. She's also worried that they won't pay out the full amount. We honor and acknowledge those feelings and acknowledge the unpleasant news that she may not get the cash at all. I pull the card underneath the Ten of Swords as an alternative to what she can do if she does indeed fail to receive the settlement in a timely manner.

The second card under the Ten of Swords is the High Priestess. "Oh, I like her. She's shiny," Becca says. "I see what this means. It is telling me that I could ask my parents for help. Maybe not for money, but I do know that they have been wanting to get rid of old furniture, seeing that I lost mine. They could help." I nod and tell her that it's a great idea. Then I honor her connection by telling her a bit more about what the High Priestess typically means.

We turn our attention to the second pile of cards on the table. I remind her what the pile stands for: "This next card represents some ideas about what you can do about your living situation." We turn this card over: it's the Page of Cups. Becca leans in and says, "Oh my, is that a fish coming out of the cup?" I look at her and say, "I don't know. What do you think it is?"

This question launches Becca into a discussion about how she sees the fish as some sort of joke, and that it represents how this disaster hasn't given her time to think about what to do. "I feel as if I'm not living in the real world," she tells me. "Everything feels so weird and strange, just like that fish in the cup."

I respond with, "Well, what does it mean when a fish is out of water?"

Becca looks at the card again. "Well, it means that the fish needs to go back to where it came from to survive. In this case, the water. Right? Since I have no house to go to, I need to find a new place."

We look at the card again, and the idea of travel pops into my head. "Maybe the fish in the cup represents a feeling you might have about moving to a new place. You said that you felt as if this was a fantasy and you had no idea where to go or what to do next, right?"

Becca stammers, "Yes, I-I am not sure where to go. This whole situation has been unreal, and I just want to start anew."

I nod and suggest that perhaps the Page of Cups is telling her that it is time to move away from her current place. I ask, "Has there been another area that you longed to live in but couldn't due to the situation of having been tied down to the house?"

"Well, now that you say it, I have wanted to move closer to my sister. My nieces just started school, and she has no one to hang out and hang around with. We've talked about me driving up there, but I have been so busy lately. Now that the house is gone and I need a new place, maybe I can stay with her for a bit and she can help me find a place and a job close by."

I look at my cell phone and realize that our time is drawing to an end. I tell her, "Okay so in this reading we drew three cards. The first card, about your settlement, doesn't look like you'll be getting the money you want but we drew a second card in case the bad news does happen. In that second card, we brainstormed ways that your family could help you out, with furniture. However, as to this new apartment… we didn't answer whether or not it's for you but instead it sounds like relocation might be better for you to be near your sister. Are you satisfied with this reading and our time together?"

Becca nods and I thank her for coming and getting a reading from me. I hand her a brochure so she can look me up easily in the future. She pays me for the reading and I reset the table and myself for the next client.

Connecting to the Global Tarot Tribe

Tarot exists where you live. If you are lucky to live in a large city, there are probably lots of local tarot-focused study groups, meetups, and events that can connect you to others with your passions. If you live in a small community or aren't ready to publicly share your love of tarot, the internet is your best place to find like-minded individuals. Being a part of a group or two (or three) can do so much for you. I highly recommend exploring your tribe options.

Communities build connections and friendships. Getting to know people is an important networking skill. You can learn a lot about the art of tarot from joining a group. You learn about new events, new decks, and even new ways to use your cards. Our tribe is filled with fun-loving, smart people and I am ever so grateful to call many of them family. There's no way I'd have developed these deep connections had I not reached out and become involved in various groups.

Communities foster innovation and new ideas. I'm in several groups, many of which regularly pose questions about card meanings, divination, and the business of being a reader. Interacting with others helps broaden our perspective, and it can change how we interact with the cards in our world. I've tested out many parts of this book at conferences, receiving feedback to make the work stronger and flow better. I've given feedback and brainstormed ideas for friends developing their own tarot-focused products. When we get together with others, the idea generation flows smoothly, so make sure you have something to note all the new ideas you'll make.

Perhaps most importantly, tarot groups give you space to learn and practice skills. Reading for others requires a certain skillset you can only develop by practicing with others. Nothing beats getting together—online or offline—to practice your readings with another person. You learn so much about the process and how to deal with different types of questions or client personalities. You'd be surprised at the number of groups catering to the art of reading and understanding card meanings.

In this section I'll share some of my favorite tips you can use to connect to the global tarot community. Believe me, there are a lot of people passionate about tarot out there. You'll learn how to find local and online communities. I'll also give you some guidelines for building a group of your own.

Types of Tribes

There are two ways you can connect with others in the tribe: locally or online. Finding like-minded people you get along with is a time-honored tradition. No matter which way you go, there is a group for you out there.

To connect with people in person, hit up the your local metaphysical stores. Many bookstores, libraries, or community colleges have boards where communities reach out to find connections. Visit these locations and see what you can find. Of importance to tarot include general interest groups, classes teaching specific techniques, and reading swaps. Select a group from the list of available postings. If nothing grabs your attention or you don't see anything going on, why not start one of your own? Skip to the section on building your own community for some ideas to get started.

The internet has changed the way we connect to people around the world. From chat rooms to forums to social media to private sites, there are lots of ways to find your personalized tarot tribe online. Running a search for tarot or divination groups in a search engine provides many interesting connections. It's a tricky decision to figure out which one is the best for you.

Whether you stick to the virtual world or in-person, you'll want to think about what types of communities you want to participate in. Think about and visualize what type of community you want to be part of to help your chances of success in finding a good fit online and off.

Here's a list of questions to get you started:

- What do you want to get out of a tarot group?

- Do you want to meet in person or stay online?

- Do you want a group of people in a specific age range?

- How skilled are you and the group? If you're starting out, do you want to connect to experienced readers? Conversely, if you're a pro, do you want to mentor those starting out on their journey?

- How specific will your group be? Do you want to find a group to practice readings with?

- How important is history? Some sites have a historical focus, versus a more intuitive approach.

Not all groups are created equal. While many associations have open membership and are ready to accept you, there are also many private ones. Some communities require payments; others require a special invitation. Other require some proof of competency level. Finding your tarot tribe takes time and the willingness to learn and be open. Of course, if you cannot locate a group of people you want to talk with, you can always start your own association to get the level of communication you want.

Learning the Group Dynamic

You've done your research and have found several ways to connect to others who enjoy tarot. This is awesome! You're on your way to making long lasting connections. At this point, you can jump right in and introduce yourself and your experience and start chatting with others. However, I've found it takes some time to understand a group's dynamic before hopping right in. It takes time to get to know people, and not everyone wants to be best friends off the start. Before you get chatting with people, I recommend you take time to listen in or look at the group's rules and regulations. Yes, even in-person groups may have their own guidelines. If you don't know what they are, ask someone.

There's a wide variety of tarot associations around the world. Some are generically dedicated to discussing tarot and all the topics associated with it (much like this book). Others have a narrow focus, selecting one aspect to delve deep into. You'll find groups dedicated to history, and some about sharing spreads both original and pre-made. There are even groups whose sole purpose is to help members buy, sell, or trade decks with others around the world.

Knowing the depth and focus of a group is important. Rules and guidelines keep members on task and focused on the overall group purpose. They can also protect member privacy from outsiders or hurtful commentary. The tarot tribe is very passionate about their decks and reading styles; most groups expect you to follow their rules. Spending the time to read through posts and discussion threads can save you time and hardship when you do join in conversations.

Tips and Tricks:

- Mind your time limits. How much time do you want to spend in the group? When locating in-person groups, make sure their meetings fit your schedule. Regarding internet groups, remember that the internet is big and social media sites can become a time sink if you let them. Beware of the vast networks and connections you can make. Safeguard your time and attentions.

- Develop empathy. People have feelings. Some-times discussions get heated and feelings get hurt. Learn to develop empathy for others and in some cases, develop a thick skin when discussing heated topics. Stick to groups that only give you infor-mative and positive interactions. Your time is too precious to spend with bitterness and contempt. Of course, you'll also want to be open to hearing opinions you don't necessarily agree with or may not have considered.

- What's your commitment level? Some groups require active participation in them, meaning you might be providing readings or reading feedback on a regular basis. Others may require you to log in or appear at meetings at regular intervals. Only you can identify what your level of engagement and boundary is. Make sure you understand what you are getting into with your groups, and be sure you can provide the quality of commitment a group may require of its members.

- Set clear boundaries. Make sure you define your own personal boundaries. Communities are diverse, filled with personalities of all types. Developing good boundaries helps you when conflicts arise. And there will be conflicts. Never let someone walk over you, or your perspectives. At the same time, allow your fellow community members have their own opinions. You are in the group to learn and share ideas on tarot.

Connecting with Others at Conferences

While the internet provides wonderful opportunities to converse with others on tarot, nothing beats attending an in-person conference. The air is electrified. You learn new techniques from superstars and get to practice what you learn with your fellow attendees. You widen your perspective on what tarot is and how it gets used. Tarot conferences occur all around the world—all you need to do is pick your destination and head out for many days of fun!

I've attended many large and small conferences occurring all over North America. Talk to your tribes and find out where the nearest conference is happening and make sure you sign up early. You may also find tarot at conferences not focused on cartomancy or Pagan interests. I've taught and attended some pop culture conferences that had panels and courses dealing with the cards as a way to promote their favorite fandoms.

In general, there are a few styles of conferences out there. One is a symposium-style, where the convention is organized by time-slots similar to a high school or college experience. At these kinds of conferences, you will have to pick a class from many different program offerings. There are hands-on workshops as well as presentations discussing other aspects of historical tarot discoveries. Symposium conferences have a whirlwind feel to them because of the wide variety of classes, teachers, and connection opportunities you have.

Another style is a larger, single class focused event. In this style of conference, everyone learns together from one or more teachers. The event may offer morning or evening break-out sessions featuring special topics you might be interested in exploring. Everyone learns the same materials at these types of events, for the most part.

No matter the format of the conference you attend, all have a few things in common: vending halls, banquets, and many chances to talk tarot and learn about the people in your tribe. Vending halls at conferences have so many neat items for purchase, from decks to cases to books and clothing—it's amazing to see the wide variety of goodies the community offers. The evening banquets are fun as well. Attendees dress in their best attire or in tarot-inspired costumes, eat a wonderful meal together, and discuss what they've learned throughout the weekend.

One you've attended a convention, and hooked up with others who share your passion, you may find yourself addicted and wanting to branch out to attend more events.

Tips and Tricks:

- Plan and budget wisely. Going to a conference isn't cheap. The closer you live to a conference, the less you spend. You need to factor in the costs of travel, hotel costs, food, and how much fun money you want to bring to spend on new decks, books, or other goodies.

- Do your research. Conferences featuring tarot happen around the globe and throughout the year. Keep a list of conferences you'd like to attend and where they are located. If the one you want has already happened, note the dates for the next year; that way, you'll have a perfect opportunity to save up and ask the coordinators questions. Many conferences have social media outreaches, too. Find them and connect to them to stay hyped through the year. Save up your money, and when you get there, immerse yourself in the experience and what it offers.

- Take care of yourself while at the conference. Conferences can get overwhelming. There are so many class choices and people; the energy is always electrified. Make sure you stay hydrated, eat two meals a day, and get at least six hours of sleep. Showers also help you relax and drain out some of the more invasive energy.

- Don't be afraid to introduce yourself to new friends or the presenters. Tarot people are the same as you and me; we all love to talk and bond over our favorite set of cards. Meeting your tribe is a big reason to attend a conference, so walk up to someone and make a new friend.

- Have an idea for a class of your own? Interact with the conference of your choice and submit your own class proposals. Organizers are always looking for fresh ideas. This is also a great way to give back to the conference and step into a leadership role.

Building Your Own Community

Whether you've been in a community for a long time or are looking to start one of your own, building a community is great way to grow your tribe. After all, getting together with others is an important social aspect for many shared passions. Taking the step to make a group takes time and some pre-planning, however.

Building a successful community has three stages:

Define what your group will bond around. Do you want to host a reading swap? Maybe a focused group deck study is more up your alley. Take the time to create a clear vision of what you want. Write down your ideas so you can clearly communicate what you do with others. This can be as simple as stating the group's goals and purpose.

Your fledgling group also needs some sort of structure to communicate and disseminate information to everyone participating. It doesn't have to be a formal system with lots of positions; it could be you teaching others and supervising various interactions for staying on target and maintaining a friendly atmosphere. If you are using an online forum, you may want to have close friends help you moderate posts and keep people on target.

Come up with an idea of success. How will you know that you've built something good if you don't know what it looks like? This can be as easy as making sure everyone stays focused and has fun. Without an idea of success, a group can lose focus and fade away.

After you've outlined the three steps for your group, figure out the logistics. Will your community exist online or offline? Do you want to put a limit on the number of people who can participate? How many moderators will you need? These are all important group planning aspects to think about.

Promoting your group is also important. Create flyers or postcards, and pass them around your local metaphysical bookstores or libraries. Use your social media outlets to broadcast your desire to find a group as well. This can generate interest around you and the people wanting to connect locally may surprise you.

Above all, have fun with your community. Your group should share successes and be a safe place for members to explore tarot and its uses.

Crafting a Vision Statement

Communities work best when they have a shared vision, whether it's the topic bringing members together or a shared goal for the future. This vision forms the basis of your tribe and can be a guiding light bringing people together. They give your community focus, purpose, and meaning. Your vision statement clues members into what you're all about and helps them decide whether or not they want to join. It can also help minimize stray conversations by reminding members of the group's function. Crafting a good vision statement takes time.

Writing a group vision statement is a great exercise. View this statement as a living document, something you can revise as the group's desire and focus shifts through time. Update it when you have new ideas and goals for the group. A good vision statement drives the engagement level of everyone in the group. The clearer your statement, the happier your community members can be.

A good vision statement clarifies the goals and sets boundaries for your community. When writing your vision statement, keep the following in mind:

Be clear and concise in your wording. "We focus our time on sharing readings and giving critiques" is more definitive than "A group for readings." The first vision statement gives potential members a glimpse into what will be expected of them. In this case, we've made a vision statement that describes a group who is dedicated to sharing readings and giving feedback on what has been written. Avoid long-winded, flowery statements that sound pretty but confuse potential members. The second statement contains too many questions: what types of readings are given? Will people be expected to receive and exchange readings? How many readings can a person post to the group? The potential for everyone wanting readings and no one wanting to give one in return could happen with a group whose description is vague.

Avoid jargon. Tarot is filled with its own lexicon and vocabulary. While jargon can give prospective members an idea of how geeky your group could be, it's not language that is widely shared. Keep those keywords out and open your community to a wider audience.

Be realistic. Your vision statement should contain requirements and goals attainable by most, if not all, the members in the group. If you are meeting in person, make sure you plan for the widest audience available.

There is no single formula for creating a good statement. If you already have friends willing to become part of your community, get feedback from them on what the vision of the group should be.

Be honest about what you want. You are shaping the form and style of your community. The vision can attract or repel people depending on their needs. No pressure, right?

Give the process some time. Keep a list of items you want to include, and re-examine the vision statement periodically. Revise and rewrite as the group dynamic changes.

Once you've got your statement down, start spreading the news. Post what you've written on your websites and use it in your promotional materials to catch the eye of potential members.

Creating a Structure

A good group requires some structure for success. This structure includes having personalized roles, meeting logistics, and adding rules to keep the flow of the group on task.

Assign group roles to help the flow of information. Depending on the amount of people your community contains these positions could be moderators who monitor online conversations for remarks and etiquette. They can keep the discussions on topic. You could also have leaders who take charge of a single meeting for each session. Rotating the leader role among all members keeps the group learning and gives everyone space to present their own perspective.

Specify clear group logistics. Where and when will the group meet? For how long? Everyone leads busy lives, so remember that not everyone will be able to attend every meeting you set up. Do your best to schedule times when a majority of members are around. Also make sure members know if there's a payment requirement to your group. Some communities use the money to secure on-site locations, or for printing handouts used in various settings. Make sure you have a central location for your in-person meet ups. Not everyone will have access to a car or be able to drive. Central locations give your members a better opportunity to visit.

Create common goals and objectives for the community. Remember, communities come together to learn and share knowledge. Giving everyone an opportunity to learn and share what they know is in your best interest. You can set theme meetings with topics that rotate from readings to spread creation. Doing so keeps the meetings fresh and your members talking.

Setting the Stage for Success

You've created a great group that is thriving. New members are showing up, and there's a lot of great discussions happening. The last thing you need to focus your attention on is creating guidelines to measure your group's status: the health, happiness, and whether or not the group lives up to the vision. We're talking gathering feedback and understanding some metrics. Not all groups will require measurements of success; however, I think setting the stage for your community's longevity and success requires ways to measure how the group is doing. When it comes down to it, does the community live up to its vision, and is it providing value to everyone?

Why should you measure the success of your group? Gathering information about what is going on in a group gives you data on your bottom line items. Using various measurements, you can make sure you're achieving the results you wanted, look at ways to improve the structure of the group, and understand what works and does not for the group as a whole. When you do not know what success looks like, you can't implement new ideas or help others understand the goals of the group you created.

There are many ways to measure your success. Think about your definition of success and use it as a baseline for the group's health. Ask other members about what their ideas of a successful group are as well. Once you have this image of what success looks like, it's easier to set group goals and achieve them.

Create periodic check-ins. Check-ins take the temperature of the group. They can find holes and locations where unrest or unease lay. These can be dates you schedule on the calendar to measure and re-evaluate the health of the group. You don't need to create much fanfare; something as simple as "How are we doing as a group?" or "Are we meeting your individual needs?" can set the stage for a wealth of feedback.

Use feedback forms to get specific comments. Especially good for getting targeted feedback about specific group activities, feedback forms can be done online or in print and can give you a wide range of information and insights into the group. Feedback forms are an invaluable tool for developing classes. It allows you to get detailed information and can be set up anonymously to protect the group as a whole.

No matter what methods you choose to develop to gain metrics regarding the health of your group, you must collaborate and act upon the ideas or plans proposed. Incorporate feedback and expand on addressing the needs of your group. You've built this community up for a purpose, and it's thriving, which is great. To keep it going, you need to be flexible and open to changes as the community grows and evolves. It's important to meet the needs of your participants, no matter the group's size and age.

I could go on and on about building connections to the global tribe, the particular groups I'm in, and more about creating great groups, but there's not enough space in this book to cover everything. There are many wonderful books, websites, and other people out there with comprehensive information. I highly recommend you do your own research when connecting to others and building communities around tarot. Let your intuition guide you. The people you meet in groups and at conferences can become wonderful collaborators and friends for life. Have fun and enjoy your connections; maybe I'll be seeing you.

For further study and reflection on the topics included in this chapter, look for the following books:

Bridges, Carol. *The Medicine Woman's Guide to Being in Business for Yourself: How to Live by Your Spiritual Vision in a Money-Based World.* Nashville, TN: Earth Nation, 1992.

Jette, Christine. *Professional Tarot: The Business of Reading, Consulting & Teaching.* St. Paul, MN: Llewellyn Publications, 2003.

Reed, Theresa. *Tarot Business in a Box.* Shorewood, WI: Self-published, 2014.

Reeves, Judy. *Writing Alone, Writing Together: A Guide for Writers and Writing Groups.* Novato, CA: New World Library, 2002.

Bibliography

Amaral, Geraldine, and Nancy Brady Cunningham. *Tarot Celebrations: Honoring the Inner Voice.* York Beach, ME: Weiser Books, 1997.

Baldwin, Christina. *Life's Companion: Journal Writing as a Spiritual Quest.* New York: Bantam Books, 1990.

Braden, Nina Lee. *Tarot for Self Discovery.* St. Paul, MN: Llewellyn Publications, 2002.

Bridges, Carol. *The Medicine Woman's Guide to Being in Business for Yourself.* Nashville, TN: Earth Nation, 1992.

Case, Paul Foster. *Tarot Fundamentals.* Accessed March 20, 2018. https://archive.org/details /PaulFosterCase-TarotFundamentals-1936.

Couturier, Andy. *Writing Open the Mind.* Berkeley, CA: Ulysses Press, 2005.

Cynova, Melissa. *Kitchen Table Tarot: Pull Up a Chair, Shuffle the Cards, and Let's Talk Tarot.* Woodbury, MN: Llewellyn Publications, 2017.

Davich, Victor. *8 Minute Meditation.* New York: Penguin, 2004.

Dominguez, Ivo Jr. *Casting Sacred Space: The Core of All Magickal Work.* San Francisco: Red Wheel/Weiser, 2012.

Elford, Jaymi. *Engaging the Spirit World.* Stafford, UK: Immanion Press, 2013.

Ellwood, Taylor. *Inner Alchemy: Energy Work and the Magic of the Body.* Stafford, UK: Immanion Press, 2006.

Fiorini, Jeanne. *Tarot Spreads & Layouts: A User's Manual for Beginning and Intermediate Readers.* Atglen, PA: Schiffer Publishing, 2010.

Galenorn, Yasmine. *Tarot Journeys: Adventures in Self-Transformation.* Kirkland, WA: Nightqueen Enterprises, 2016.

Giles, Cynthia. *The Tarot: History, Mystery, and Lore.* New York: Fireside Books, 1992.

———. *The Tarot: Methods, Mastery, and More.* New York: Fireside Books, 1996.

Graham, Sasha. *365 Tarot Spells: Creating the Magic in Each Day.* Woodbury, MN: Llewellyn Publications, 2016.

Greer, Mary K. *Tarot for Your Self.* Van Nuys, CA: Newcastle Publishing Company, 1987.

Heidrick, Bill. "Tarot Meditations 1975–76." http://
hermetic.com/heidrick/Tarot_meditations
.html.

Huggens, Kim. *Tarot 101: Mastering the Art of Reading the
Cards*. Woodbury, MN: Llewellyn Publications, 2010.

Jette, Christine. *Professional Tarot: The Business of Reading,
Consulting & Teaching*. St. Paul, MN: Llewellyn Publications, 2003.

———. *Tarot for All Seasons: Celebrating the Days & Nights
of Power*. St. Paul, MN: Llewellyn Publications, 2001.

———. *Tarot Shadow Work*. St. Paul, MN: Llewellyn Publications, 2000.

Johnson, Cait. *Tarot for Every Day: Ideas and Activities for
Bringing Tarot Wisdom into Your Daily Life*. Wappingers,
NY: Shawangunk Press, 1994.

Katz, Marcus. *Tarosophy: Tarot to Engage Life, Not Escape It*.
Chaing Mai, Thailand: Salamander and Sons, 2011

Kenner, Corrine. *Tarot for Writers*. Woodbury, MN:
Llewellyn Publications, 2009.

———. *Tarot Journaling: Using the Celtic Cross to Unveil
Your Hidden Story*. St. Paul, MN: Llewellyn Publications,
2006.

Kraig, Donald Michael. *Tarot & Magic*. St. Paul, MN:
Llewellyn Publications, 2002.

Leon, Dai. *Origins of the Tarot: Cosmic Evolution and the Principles of Immortality.* Berkeley, CA: Frog Books, 2009.

McElroy, Mark. *What's in the Cards for You?.* St. Paul, MN: Llewellyn Publications, 2005.

Michelsen, Teresa. *Designing Your Own Tarot Spreads.* St. Paul, MN: Llewellyn Publications, 2003.

Moore, Barbara. *Tarot Spreads: Layouts & Techniques to Empower Your Readings.* Woodbury, MN: Llewellyn Publications, 2012.

Morgan, Michele. *A Magical Course in Tarot: Reading the Cards in a Whole New Way.* Berkeley, CA: Conari Press, 2002.

Morrison, Dorothy. *Everyday Tarot Magic: Meditation & Spells.* St. Paul, MN: Llewellyn Publications, 2002.

Pollack, Rachel. *Tarot Wisdom: Spiritual Teachings and Deeper Meanings.* St. Paul, MN: Llewellyn Publications, 2003.

Polson, Willow. *The Veil's Edge: Exploring the Boundaries of Magic.* New York: Kensington Publishing, 2003.

Powell, Robert, trans. *Meditations on the Tarot: A Journey into Christian Hermeticism.* New York: Penguin Group, 1985.

Quinn, Paul. *Tarot for Life: Reading the Cards for Everyday Guidance and Growth.* Wheaton, IL: Quest Books, 2009.

Reed, Theresa. *Tarot Business in a Box.* Shorewood, WI: Self-published, 2014.

Reeves, Judy. *Writing Alone, Writing Together: A Guide for Writers and Writing Groups.* Novato, CA: New World Library, 2002.

Renee, Janina. *Tarot Spells.* St. Paul, MN: Llewellyn Publications, 1990.

Sim, Valerie. *Tarot Outside the Box.* St. Paul, MN: Llewellyn Publications, 2004.

Tyson, Donald. *Portable Magic: Tarot Is the Only Tool You Need.* St. Paul, MN: Llewellyn Publications. 2006.

Webster, Richard. *Pendulum Magic for Beginners.* Woodbury, MN: Llewellyn Publications, 2011.

Wen, Benebell. *Holistic Tarot: An Integrative Approach to Using Tarot for Personal Growth.* Berkeley, CA: North Atlantic Books, 2015.

To Write the Author

If you wish to contact the author or would like more information about this book, please write to the author in care of Llewellyn Worldwide, and we will forward your request. Both the author and the publisher appreciate hearing from you and learning of your enjoyment of this book and how it has helped you. Llewellyn Worldwide cannot guarantee that every letter written to the author can be answered, but all will be forwarded. Please write to:

Jaymi Elford
℅ Llewellyn Worldwide
2143 Wooddale Drive
Woodbury, MN 55125-2989

Please enclose a self-addressed stamped envelope for reply,
or $1.00 to cover costs. If outside the USA, enclose
an international postal reply coupon.

www.llewellyn.com

GET MORE AT LLEWELLYN.COM

Visit us online to browse hundreds of our books and decks, plus sign up to receive our e-newsletters and exclusive online offers.

- **Free tarot readings • Spell-a-Day • Moon phases**
- **Recipes, spells, and tips • Blogs • Encyclopedia**
- **Author interviews, articles, and upcoming events**

GET SOCIAL WITH LLEWELLYN

Find us on 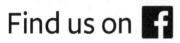  @LlewellynBooks

www.Facebook.com/LlewellynBooks

GET BOOKS AT LLEWELLYN

LLEWELLYN ORDERING INFORMATION

Order online: Visit our website at www.llewellyn.com to select your books and place an order on our secure server.

Order by phone:
- Call toll free within the US at 1-877-NEW-WRLD (1-877-639-9753)
- We accept VISA, MasterCard, American Express, and Discover.
- Canadian customers must use credit cards.

Order by mail:
Send the full price of your order (MN residents add 6.875% sales tax) in US funds plus postage and handling to: Llewellyn Worldwide, 2143 Wooddale Drive, Woodbury, MN 55125-2989

POSTAGE AND HANDLING

STANDARD (US):
(Please allow 12 business days)
$30.00 and under, add $6.00.
$30.01 and over, FREE SHIPPING.

INTERNATIONAL ORDERS,
INCLUDING CANADA:
$16.00 for one book, plus $3.00 for each additional book.

Visit us online for more shipping options.
Prices subject to change.

FREE CATALOG!

To order, call
1-877-
NEW-WRLD
ext. 8236
or visit our
website

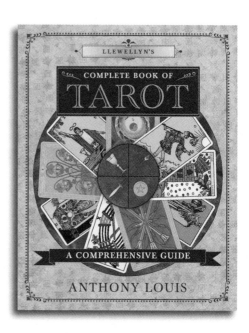

LLEWELLYN'S

COMPLETE BOOK OF

TAROT

A COMPREHENSIVE GUIDE

ANTHONY LOUIS

Llewellyn's Complete Book of Tarot
A Comprehensive Guide
ANTHONY LOUIS

This book covers everything about tarot and includes references for readers who want to go deeper into a particular topic: History, various types of tarot, associations and correspondences, reversals, dignities, spreads, reading tips, card meanings, and activities. Author Anthony Louis provides the information with clarity and style.

978-0-7387-4908-2, 336 pp., 8 x 10   **$24.99**
